The Management of
Pacific Marine Resources

Also of Interest

Making Ocean Policy: The Politics of Government Organization and Management, edited by Francis W. Hoole, Robert L. Friedheim, and Timothy M. Hennessey

Resource Management and the Oceans: The Political Economy of Deep Seabed Mining, Kurt Michael Shusterich

Managing Ocean Resources: A Primer, edited by Robert L. Friedheim

Georges Bank: Past, Present, and Future of a Marine Environment, edited by Guy C. McLeod and John H. Prescott

Coastal Aquaculture Law and Policy: A Case Study of California, Gerald Bowden

International Ocean Shipping: Current Concepts and Principles, Bernhard J. Abrahamsson

Superships and Nation-States: The Transnational Politics of The Intergovernmental Maritime Consultative Organization, Harvey B. Silverstein

Aquaculture Development in Less Developed Countries: Social, Economic, and Political Problems, edited by Leah J. Smith and Susan Peterson

Aquaculture Economics: Basic Concepts and Methods of Analysis, Yung C. Shang

Westview Special Studies in Ocean Science and Policy

The Management of Pacific Marine Resources: Present Problems and Future Trends
John P. Craven

The mineral, food, and energy potential of the oceans increases in importance as land-based resources approach their ultimate limits. International planning for the utilization of common ocean areas beyond territorial waters has thus become a vital task, one made difficult by competition among nations and the unregulated operations of multinational companies.

As a senior adviser to the U.S. delegation at UNCLOS III (Third UN Conference on the Law of the Sea), Dr. Craven provides an expert look at the full range of ocean resources and an insider's view of UN negotiations on common areas of the Pacific Ocean. His book is essential reading for those interested in the future uses of the oceans and in who will benefit from the bounty.

John P. Craven, an ocean engineer and lawyer, was chief scientist of the Polaris system and promoted the first successful U.S. experiment in generating usable energy from the thermal gradient in tropical ocean waters. He is now dean of Marine Programs at the University of Hawaii, marine affairs coordinator for the state of Hawaii, and director of the Law of the Sea Institute.

Published in cooperation with
The Hubert H. Humphrey Institute of Public Affairs
University of Minnesota, Minneapolis, Minnesota

Pacific Basin Project, Publication #1

The Management of Pacific Marine Resources: Present Problems and Future Trends

John P. Craven

Foreword by Harlan Cleveland

Westview Press / Boulder, Colorado

Westview Special Studies in Ocean Science and Policy

Copyright © 1982 by Hubert H. Humphrey Institute of Public Affairs

Published in 1982 in the United States of America by
 Westview Press, Inc.
 5500 Central Avenue
 Boulder, Colorado 80301
 Frederick A. Praeger, President and Publisher

Library of Congress Cataloging in Publication Data
Craven, John P.
 The management of Pacific marine resources.
 (Westview special studies in ocean science and policy) (Pacific basin project; publication #1)
 "Published in cooperation with the Hubert H. Humphrey Institute of Public Affairs, University of Minnesota, Minneapolis, Minnesota"—p. iv.
 Includes index.
 1. Marine resources—Pacific Ocean. I. Title. II. Series. III. Series: Pacific basin project; publication #1.
 GC1023.885.C73 1982   333.91'64   82-8442
 ISBN 0-86531-424-1   AACR2

Printed and bound in the United States of America

Contents

Maps and Tables

Foreword:
The Pacific Basin
and the Law of the Sea

In the late 1970s a sudden wave of organizational enthu-
siasm crested for various projects concerning the Pacific.
Japan's Prime Minister (1979–80) Masayoshi Ohira initially
envisioned the concept of a "Pacific Community" and dis-
covered a mutually interested party in Australia's Prime Minister, Malcolm Fraser. In fact, Australia sponsored the first in
a series of seminars about a Pacific Community of nations.
Meanwhile, in the United States, congressional committees
compiled reports and held hearings on Ohira's Pacific Community idea.

In the structure of world order the technologically strong
are usually the first to demand and establish organization and
institutions. The technologically weak — the developing
nations — customarily react with apprehension, fearing that
the strong want to freeze their comparative strength. So it
was with the Pacific Community. A Korean described the
concept as "a prematurely born child." Voices from ASEAN
(the Association of Southeast Asian Nations), protective of
their newly valued subregional cooperation, were fiercely
cautious about what one of their spokesmen called "pro-
moting a generalized Community."

In the Western Pacific and East Asia, wartime Japan's
Greater East Asian Co-Prosperity Sphere still lives in

Portions of this foreword were previously published. See Harlan
Cleveland, "The Libyan Episode and the Great Sea Grab," *The Christian
Science Monitor*, 21 August 1981, p. 22, © 1981 by Harlan Cleveland, all
rights reserved.

memory. Forty years later, another coprosperity sphere, even if promoted by certifiably democratic politicians in Japan, Australia, and the United States, still recalls too many disturbing overtones. Just now, it seems, every U.S., Japanese, or Australian drumbeat for new Pacific-wide political institutions intensifies the polite-but-firm, passive resistance of the Pacific's "South"—ASEAN, the Pacific islands, the Republic of Korea, and the two parts of a still divided China.

Meanwhile, two independent American institutes engaged in policy research have remained deeply interested in the future of the Pacific—the Aspen Institute for Humanistic Studies and the University of Minnesota's newly expanded Hubert H. Humphrey Institute of Public Affairs. Together they envisioned a new approach to the Pacific Community, namely, to set aside for the time being the issue of political organization in the Pacific Basin and begin instead with the underlying questions: What concrete problems need to be tackled, what functions need to be performed that might require new forms of international consultation, cooperation, coordination, parallel national action, or common action by communities-of-the-concerned in the Pacific Basin?

Until there is some consensus about what has to be done and by whom, the questions raised by "Pacific Community" in its generalized form are indeed unanswerable because prematurely political. A political question like "Which countries should be 'members' of a Pacific Community?" can be addressed only in the context of the functional questions: What action is required, and which countries are in a position to do what about it? To answer these questions, the Pacific Basin Project was born, a joint venture of the Aspen and Humphrey institutes.

Our plan of attack was first to consider, in a series of multinational but nongovernmental workshops, four functional fields in which a thicker web of Pacific-wide cooperation might turn out to be needed: (1) the management of Pacific marine resources, (2) the changing industrial geography of the Pacific Basin, (3) the prospects for food and development, and (4) the Pacific impact of the communications/information revolution.

The first workshop, on marine resources, was held in Tokyo in June 1981.[1] It was cosponsored and hosted by the International House of Japan, and the program was organized by the author of this book.

The book itself grew directly out of the workshop. It is partly based on substantial contributions from several workshop participants — political scientist Roger Benjamin, adjunct member of the Humphrey Institute faculty and associate dean of the College of Liberal Arts at the University of Minnesota; Choung Il Chee, international fisheries expert from Korea; Edgar Gold, a Canadian expert on maritime transportation; Michael Hirschfeld, a businessman from New Zealand, who served as workshop rapporteur; Kent Keith, deputy director of the State of Hawaii's Department of Planning and Economic Development; Frances Lai, a political scientist at the National University of Singapore; Masataka Watanabe, National Institute for Environmental Studies in Tsukuba, Japan; and Peter Wilson, an adviser to the government of Papua New Guinea.

This book is not, however, a consensus report or a meeting summary — in my experience such consensus writings have often been bland and uninteresting, and what John Craven has pulled together in this book is neither. He is one of the world's most original thinkers in both ocean science and ocean law. An ocean engineer and lawyer by training, John Craven has been chief scientist of the Polaris program, a professor at M.I.T., author of *Ocean Engineering Systems*, and for the past decade dean of Marine Programs at the University of Hawaii, marine affairs coordinator for the governor of Hawaii, and director of the International Law of the Sea Institute, which is based in Honolulu. His perception of the oceans' future management is far from conventional, but is grounded in competent, thorough scholarship and an educated intuition.

*   *   *

Amidst all the rhetoric of the 1970s about a fairer international order, there was only one real negotiation about structural change in the global system. That was the long-running

Third United Nations Conference on the Law of the Sea, nicknamed UNCLOS III. Its starting point was a 1970 U.N. General Assembly resolution, endorsed by the United States, declaring the oceans to be "the common heritage of mankind." Yet the one subject on which, after more than a decade, consensus has eluded the marathon negotiators is the governance of the ocean commons.

"What happened to the ocean commons?" A professor from Singapore answered her own rhetorical question at the Tokyo workshop: "They put the cake on the table, and the cake disappeared." Eighty-nine of the 120 coastal nations have already staked out 200-mile Exclusive Economic Zones, and the world is reacting as though these zones are both legal and policeable. The EEZs may well become legal, by custom if not by treaty. Most of them will never be policeable.

The long-running ocean law talks (one expert calls them "an international version of single-issue politics") have thus been partly channeled into declarations of national jurisdiction, if not control, of most of the traditional marine resources. The resulting bonanza, except for smaller payoffs here and there (around the Pacific islands, for example), is mainly for the account of the already affluent nations.

In the short run, the most important consequence of the "sea grab" will be to move into national jurisdictions 90 percent of the ocean's fish. Even the "highly migratory species" — such as Pacific tuna and salmon which cavalierly ignore the lines man carefully draws in the water — are being subjected to national jurisdiction. Congress has now legislated that salmon spawned in U.S. rivers carry their American citizenship wherever they swim. But the Coast Guard, even if reinforced by the FBI's computers and the U.S. Navy's gunships, can never catch up with most of the trawlers operated by foreigners who catch made-in-America salmon as they swim in the open seas.

The "sea grab" has also nationalized most of the Pacific's remaining known deposits of offshore oil and gas. But the richest deposits of those other exotic minerals, the manganese nodules, are on the deep seabed, still part of the Pacific "commons."

Seabed mining of manganese nodules—the favored "claims" are under Pacific waters—seemed "just around the corner" a decade ago. Today the block has been extended, hence the distance to that corner has lengthened. The key constraint is uncertainty about the rules of the game. Efforts by the United States and other high-technology nations to write their own rules may not completely satisfy the great international companies that must contemplate not only the investment of a billion dollars per operation, but also making the investment without certainty in laying claim to the resulting product. The potential for conflict in the absence of internationally accepted ground rules may deter the oil giants and others for whom seabed mining, potentially large as it will be some day, is only a sideline today. The current absence of high demand for some of the minerals involved (nickel, copper, and cobalt) is also slowing things down.

The outcomes of UNCLOS III will not much affect the profitable future of Pacific shipping. But despite resistance from shipowning nations, especially Japan, a pattern of tighter regulation is likely to develop in other contexts—IMCO (Inter-Governmental Maritime Consultative Organization) controls on vessel safety and vessel-based pollution, and UNCTAD (United Nations Conference on Trade and Development) campaigns against "flags of convenience." Moreover, systems of marine traffic control are overdue for modernization; they are technically several decades behind the comparable systems for air traffic control.

*   *   *

A major new factor in Pacific Basin development—so new that its governance was not really considered in the Law of the Sea negotiations—will be ocean thermal energy conversion (OTEC).

This idea, proved out in Hawaii's "mini-OTEC" experiment only two years ago, is that substantial differences in temperature between the ocean surface and deep waters can be converted into useful energy by pumping the cold water to the surface. The electricity such a system makes possible can be used either directly for operations based at sea or on nearby islands, or indirectly for powering the production of transportable fuel (synthetic fuel from sea-borne coal, or hydrogen from seawater, as examples).

Although there will eventually be applications of OTEC in many parts of the world, it is quintessentially a "Southern" and a Pacific resource. Most of the best places for OTEC, which needs five thousand to six thousand feet of depth and will be optimal in tropical waters, are either clearly in the high seas commons or in the claimed economic jurisdictions of developing countries including—and especially—islands in the South Pacific. OTEC does not have to be a large central system; the resource could be adapted to the power needs of an island nation or a large (e.g., synthetic fuel) operation.

The thermal-conversion potentials are theoretically enormous. In the world's oceans, between latitudes of twenty degrees on either side of the equator, some 1,000 quads (quadrillion British thermal units) per year are quietly unexploited today—three times the current world demand for energy and perhaps one-third of the world energy demand 100 years from now.

OTEC, like other forms of "solar" energy, will probably have a lengthy developmental time frame. The time span depends more upon projected need than technology. Undoubtedly we will have to look at least twenty years ahead for significant development of all the really important alternatives to oil as the world's dominant energy source. (The one exception is conservation, which can be effected right away.) If development does not start now, we will still be overdependent on the dwindling oil supply even in the first part of the twenty-first century.

The environmental effects of OTEC are positive. In Tokyo a Japanese expert sketched for us how the nutrients brought up from the deep sea along with the cold water could be used to produce biomass that could be the basis for producing more energy (in the form of methane) or food from aquaculture. The nutrients brought up as an OTEC by-product could be an environmental problem—for example, by inducing eutrophication in an enclosed sea. But they might better be considered as the basis for a new technology-based biomass industry. (That still leaves some interesting uncertainties. If nutrients are brought up from the deep-ocean commons, who is entitled to the resulting biomass, who owns the resulting methane?)

Although, as noted, energy from the ocean thermal gradient is an inherently "Southern" resource, it can be exploited only by advanced technology from the Northern Hemisphere's industrialized nations. Inside the 200-mile zones, the development of ocean energy can be regulated by national laws (as in the OTEC operations now being planned by the Japanese for Okinawa and by General Electric, Lockheed, TRW Inc., and the local utility for Hawaii) or by arrangements between the island "owners" of the warm tropical waters and those who have the technology and capital to take energy from the thermal gradient.

On the high seas, some international rules of the game will sooner or later be necessary to regulate OTEC "grazing rights." One workshop participant went further: he suggested a "Commons Agency" to develop OTEC, a partnership between those who might invest in the system and the residents of the tropical regions in which it will have to be developed. (See Appendix C—the Chee Plan.) The idea found an interested audience. It might help the equity equation, said another conferee from a developing country: "The EEZs mostly help the developed countries. Maybe the ocean commons can be some use to the rest of us."

*   *   *

Futurists have been forecasting a "Pacific century." To participants in our Tokyo workshop, the long-run prospects for the Pacific Basin were hard to be pessimistic about if we were willing to look a generation ahead.

The central problem for the Pacific region today is all too obvious: its great dependence on Middle East oil and Atlantic products, squeezing through the narrow choke points of Malacca and Panama. With modern technologies and a generation of time, the Pacific Basin contains sufficient resources to erase the region's energy deficit.

Meanwhile more and more Pacific nations will be moving — they already are moving — from the periphery to the center of communications and information flows. The rapid development of educated peoples and rural enterprise already points to an era of food adequacy without undue dependence on the great world granaries (which also rim the Pacific). The message of overpopulation has gotten through, including to China. In one generation, without war, there should be no "poor nations" lapped by the Pacific Ocean.

In the future, sharing an ocean will be at least as significant a basis for cooperation as sharing a landmass. Oceans have traditionally been regarded as separating countries and peoples from each other. Today, however, it may be more sensible to view oceans as a primary means of bringing functional partners together for development, prosperity, security, and peace. For the Pacific Basin countries, the world's largest ocean forms the basis for this expanded cooperative sphere.

Harlan Cleveland
Director, Hubert H. Humphrey
Institute of Public Affairs,
University of Minnesota

Acknowledgments

Special thanks are due to Mikio Kato, program director of the International House of Japan; Harlan Cleveland, director of the Hubert H. Humphrey Institute of Public Affairs; Joseph E. Slater, president of the Aspen Institute for Humanistic Studies; and the Tokyo workshop participants for their kind participation in and sponsorship of this book.

Special thanks are also due to D. K. Schaff for editing, to Kathleen Ganley for typing the final manuscript, and to Gregory Chu of the University of Minnesota Cartographic Laboratory for creating our maps.

J.P.C.

1
The Unsettled Law of the Sea

The widely held belief that the seas and their resources are a commons to be shared by all peoples derives its plausibility from the facts of nature, not from international treaties and compacts. Indeed, the history of treaties and compacts has been one of continuous but unsuccessful attempts to partition the seemingly infinite oceans into finite units of sovereignty. From the Boatman's Code of the recorded laws of Hammurabi in 1750 B.C. through the Papal Bull of 1493, from the Mare Clausum of Selden in 1610 to the 1958 Geneva Convention of the Law of the Sea, the realities of the maritime environment have made these legal agreements, and many others, ineffectual.

Even with the advanced technologies now available it is a daunting consideration that the oceans can, and in fact, must, be managed. This essay reviews the major issues associated with the development of management policy related to the oceans, particularly the Pacific. Whether the Pacific Marine Commons will become more rather than less of the common heritage of the world's peoples is the question addressed. The Pacific Ocean as a resource offers humankind incalculable potential benefits. However, the fate to be apprehended is some new but as yet unenvisioned oceanic version of the "tragedy of the commons"[2] — a tragedy which is indeed so often present in the history of land-based developments.

The newest attempt to establish a legal regime for the oceans is embodied in the current text of the Third United Nations Conference on the Law of the Sea (UNCLOS III). It suggests a dramatic change in the free and common use of the oceans. High seas freedoms remain unabridged only in areas 200 miles distant from the nearest continent or inhabitable islands, and in the deep oceans only in the water column above the seabed.

A very large part of the "common heritage" has been chopped up into 12-mile territorial seas, 24-mile contiguous zones, 200-mile Exclusive Economic Zones (EEZs), and "definitions" of the continental shelf that run it out to 350 miles and as deep as 2,500 meters below the surface, depending on the geological formation. (See Figure 1 for illustration of the EEZs.)

Although the UNCLOS text has yet to be formalized, there are many who maintain that major portions of the text have already become the international law of the sea. Many nations have made unilateral, bilateral, and regional assertions of rights and duties which more or less conform to the treaty. The pervasive notion of UNCLOS and of the developed nations is that the new Law of the Sea has, in fact, terminated the commons status of the ocean except for navigation, military use, and limited forms of fishing. But there are competing views advanced by the Third World countries to the effect that United Nations resolutions have made the resources of the seas the common heritage (and thus the common property) of humankind and that they cannot be legally harvested without formal consent by the peoples of the world (i.e., the United Nations). Socialist lawyers have argued that the seabed is *res communes*[3] and cannot be utilized without the mutual assent of socialist nations. Thus only the industrialized democracies have maintained that the current status of the seabed and its resources is *res nullius,*[4] but their view has prevailed in practice—for now.

The long and unsuccessful past efforts at regulating the oceans make it naive to believe that UNCLOS can readily accomplish what its predecessors could not. Indeed, there are infinite challenges and potential challenges to the letter and the spirit of the UNCLOS text. Already a pattern is emerging of overt, covert, and negotiated violations of treaty provisions. The violations are probably most flagrant with respect to fisheries, but are also occurring in the dumping of wastes

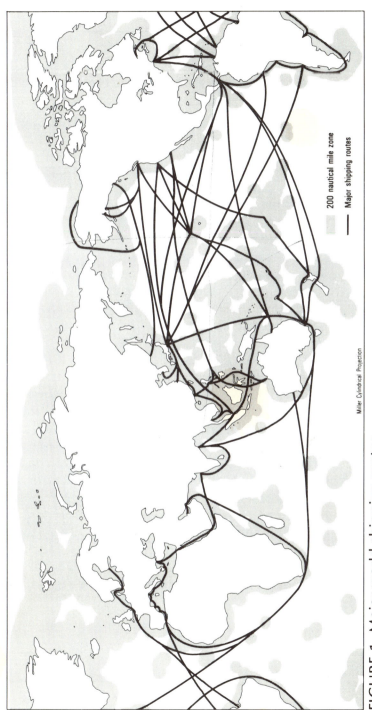

200 nautical mile zone

Major shipping routes

Miller Cylindrical Projection

FIGURE 1 Major world shipping routes

into the ocean, noncompliance with flag state and port state pollution laws, and illegal entry of goods and people.

Realistic projections of the future of the oceans as a commons should not be predicated on the UNCLOS text alone, but should include an analysis of international actors (non-signatory nations, multinational corporations, international and regional organizations) and the threats they can pose to legal regimes (economic coercion; clandestine, open, or negotiated violation; piracy, misinterpretation, perceived threats to security) in relation to the full spectrum of ocean uses (transportation, military, fishing, energy, mineral extraction, waste disposal, etc.).

The potential combination of actors, threats, and ocean uses defies examination in a finite treatise. What will be reported here is an examination of some potentially dominant uses of the ocean in the Pacific Basin. This examination was made in a workshop in Tokyo, during the last week of June 1981, on "The Management of the Pacific Marine Commons."[5] The workshop participants recognized that the current use of the Pacific Ocean is as a medium for transportation and for the projection of military might. However, they concluded that in the future, the processing and transport of energy, together with the extraction of mineral and food resources, will constitute the dominant use of the sea.

These uses of the Pacific Commons were analyzed on the following cumulative assumptions: (1) that the United Nations treaty and/or its provisions will soon be in place as the international norm; (2) that regional arrangements in conformance with the treaty will, nonetheless, produce regional regimes that may largely nullify the intents of the treaty; and (3) that attempts by noncooperative international entities to avoid the restraints and duties imposed by the treaty will be widespread.

2
Energy Futures of the Oceans

To understand the relationship of energy to the oceans, we must view the current near-term predictions of the world energy situation as shortsighted. In the past four thousand years the world has made major shifts in its dominant forms of energy utilization. The initial development was that of wood as a fuel for heat, solar energy as wind for motive power at sea, and biomass in the form of fodder for animal power. The first major transition, from the middle to the end of the nineteenth century, was to coal as the fuel for ships and trains and the major fuel for electricity. The second transition, beginning in the 1920s, shifted coal to third place behind oil and gas, resulting in our current world dependence on these increasingly scarce resources.

We are now experiencing the beginnings of the next transition. These beginnings signal a return to coal in order to produce electricity and synthetic fuels (synfuel). But the new shift will have to go further; the transition will have to be more fundamental. One hundred years from now the world could consume 3,000 quads (3×10^{18} BTU) of energy per year even if world per-capita consumption would be only two-thirds of current U.S. per-capita consumption, if population control techniques would have proved successful, and if conservation would be extensively practiced. This would compare with the current world consumption of about 300 quads per year. Thus, all possible forms of energy will be required to meet this enormous demand; the production of this energy will entail the fullest development of such solar techniques as ocean thermal energy, possibly in combination with nuclear fusion. *It is thus a central assumption of this analysis*

*that the transition to new energy forms must be well under-
way in the next fifty to one hundred years and that new energy sources such as ocean thermal energy (OTEC) will
become the dominant forms of production.*

Students of world energy may find the emphasis on OTEC
to be in conflict with current consensus. Indeed it is a thesis
of this text that OTEC has been neglected, but that it *cannot*
be much longer neglected.

Conventional Sources: Oil and Coal

Although the initial stages of transition to new forms of
energy have already begun, reliance must still be placed on
coal and oil throughout the remainder of this century and beyond. Primary reliance upon ocean transportation will insure
adequate supplies of these resources.

The Pacific Ocean's role in the development of coal as an
energy resource had its beginnings in the nineteenth century.
The most historically significant effect of the utilization of
coal was the choice made by the United States to employ
Hawaii, Guam, and the Philippines as sites for coaling stations. Concurrently Britain, France, and Germany established their own separate stepping stones in the Gilberts,
Samoa, Hong Kong, Fiji, the New Hebrides, Tahiti, the Marshalls, and the Carolines. As oil replaced coal, the coaling
stations all but disappeared, and today the role of the Pacific
and other oceans in the development of oil resources is of
more immediate interest.

Geologists recognize that the landmasses of the world were
once a single continent, which later was fractured by movement of the world's tectonic plates (partly subcontinental and
partly suboceanic) (like the cooling crusts of a "baked
Alaska"). The sediments slumping and washing into the sea
from the separating continents enriched the marine organic
deposits already there, and as the plates were subjected to
folding, pinchouts, and doming, oil was entrapped from
decaying organic deposits. Thus the world's major oil fields
will be and are in current or former coastal regions, the continental shelves, or shallow seas. A look at Figure 2 will show

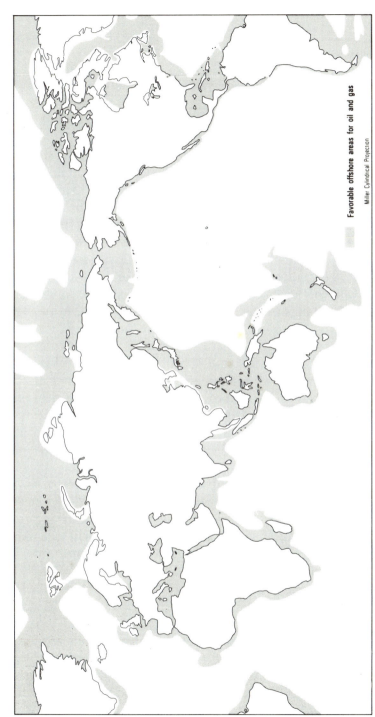

Favorable offshore areas for oil and gas

Miller Cylindrical Projection

FIGURE 2 Favorable offshore areas for oil and gas

where these major oil deposits are, or are believed to be — the Middle East, Alaska's North Slope, the Persian Gulf, the Indonesian archipelago, the Yellow Sea, the China Sea, and probably the Mediterranean, the offshore shelves of Angola and Brazil, and the separation zone between Argentina and the Antarctic.

Any illusions that the oil and gas on the continental shelves would be available as the common heritage of humankind were shattered by the Truman declaration of 1946, which declared U.S. sovereignty over its continental shelf for the purpose of exploiting oil and gas. The UNCLOS treaty embeds this nationalist notion in international law with a complex continental shelf formula. The small, site-specific, and nonmobile character of continental-shelf oil fields is compatible with this legal regime. But it is not a foregone conclusion that this establishes the legal status of offshore oil. A number of areas are in dispute. For example, the status of such uninhabited or rarely inhabited islands as the Tiuyutais or Senkakus, the Paracels, the Spratleys, and the Banjos, has raised differences of opinion on whether these islands affect the legal status of the seabed. The status of the shelf near the Antarctic continent is also in doubt. The signatories to the Antarctic treaty are but a fraction of the international community. The treaty is deliberately ambiguous as to whether sovereignty exists for any part of the Antarctic shelf — despite the fact that, or perhaps because, several signatories have claimed sovereignty. In either the semienclosed sea, or in Antarctica itself, the presence of a drilling rig carrying the flag of any nation would cause an international dilemma (which might nonetheless result in international inaction).

Even taking these complexities into account, few observers would be rash enough to predict that the development of offshore oil will not follow the pattern proposed by UNCLOS.

The transportation, processing, and storage of oil present other issues. The scale of economic transport, requiring the use of deep-draft supertankers, has greatly constrained the routes of energy commerce in the ocean. Oil from the Persian Gulf must pass through the Straits of Hormuz with Iran on the East Bank and the tiny Emirate of Oman on the West. Oil bound for the east coast of the American continent must pass through the economic zone of the Malagasy Republic and round the southern tip of Africa. Oil bound for Japan and the west coast of America must pass through the Straits of Malacca with Malaysia on the north, Indonesia on the south, and Singapore guarding the eastern portal. There are no practical transit alternatives to using these straits. The Sunda and Lombok alternatives are too shallow. Even Malacca is so shallow that deep-draft vessels and tankers often find their bottoms in the silt, and tankers are encouraged to utilize local pilots to ensure a successful transit.

The industrialized nations have been successful in establishing a transit passage regime through traditional straits (including Gibraltar). Nonetheless, states bordering the straits have a number of legal means to regulate or deny transit—for example, in the language on pollution in the UNCLOS treaty draft or in the language of a straits regime itself. These states would reap great political and economic benefits if they could regulate and charge tolls for passage through the straits. Indeed, political and economic lures have been a factor in persuading these states to accede to the proposed UNCLOS regime. When the price paid to maintain unimpeded transit is inadequate, states bordering the straits will have both the legal justification and the physical capability to regulate passage.

The perceived necessity for strategic oil reserves has added a new element in the use of the oceans as a commons. The maintenance of oil reserves, which will last from two months to two years, is a goal of most oil-dependent states. Japan has developed a novel and cost-effective method of storage by using surplus tankers that drift on the high seas. Western nations have followed suit. Standby power is available, and a continuous navigation and radar watch is maintained so that each ship can be underway in time to avoid navigation interference in prohibited waters. (Although calculations of ship density and response time indicate that these operations should be perfectly safe, these ships are, in fact, not under control for an hour or more after an initial alert.)

The incentives for regional or basin cooperation in the production and distribution of energy are highly dependent on the nature and source of energy flow. Presently, the dominant energy flow for the Western Pacific is from the Middle East through the Straits of Malacca. Indonesia and Malaysia are major producers of crude oil, and one would expect that these countries would be major consumers of their own products and that the ASEAN nations would be major importers of this regionally generated energy resource. Such is not the case. The economic pull from the Western Pacific and the West Coast of the United States is so great that the ASEAN nations import the vast majority of their crude from the Middle East and export the bulk of their production to Japan, the United States, and the Western Pacific. Thus Indonesia exports 90 percent of its crude to Japan, the United States, and Trinidad; Malaysia's domestic consumption is mainly met from Middle East imports (90,000 b/d) and its domestic production (260,000 b/d) is mainly export-oriented. The dependence of the Western Pacific on Mideastern oil and the resulting exclusion of the Malaccan strait states (Thailand, Indonesia, Singapore, Taiwan, and Korea) from a proportionate share of the energy inhibits regional and Pacific Basin cooperation and places a high premium on placating the Middle Eastern producers. J. F. Kirk, in a paper on "Energy Problems and Growth Prospects of the Pacific Basin," has highlighted the significance of the energy deficit of the Western Pacific and its dependence on transit through the straits and an assured supply of Mideast crude. He emphasizes that quite a different situation exists or will exist in the Eastern Pacific as a result of Mexican, Alaskan, and California crudes. This region can become a net exporter in the near future, alleviating the straits dependence of the Western Pacific. Kirk also points out that energy needs of the year 2000 will not be met unless there is a substantial development of synthetic fuels:

Coal is projected to be a major source of energy supply growth, replacing oil and gas in major industrial and electric utility markets and meeting a substantial share of new energy demand. Coal use is projected to grow almost three percent per year, marginally increasing its share of world energy supply from its present 26 percent to 28 percent by the year 2000. Including coal converted to synthetic oil and gas, coal's share in 2000 would increase to 30 percent and rival oil as the largest single source of energy.[6]

Kirk's projection for reducing the energy deficit in the Western Pacific Basin is highly dependent on the expanded development of coal-derived synthetic fuels and, in particular, the use of Australian coal. He concludes that the combination of Australian coal and oil from the Eastern Pacific should reduce dependence on Middle East oil from 65 percent in 1980 to 40 percent in the year 2000. A continuation of such a trend could form the basis for increased Western Pacific Basin cooperation and decrease the significance of the straits. Greater cohesion among the ASEAN nations would require cooperation in the development of the China and Yellow seas, as no other viable long-term fossil fuel alternative would be available to them.

The major inhibitions to realizing the energy scenario envisioned by Kirk are the costs and the technical problems associated with the development of synthetic fuel from coal. A National Academy of Engineering Report ("Refining Synthetic Liquids from Coal and Shale") cites the need for a source of carbon-free hydrogen as the key to the large-scale development of synthetic fuel. Producing hydrogen on such a scale is within the capabilities of OTEC.

Ocean Thermal Energy Conversion (OTEC)

Potential energy sources for the production of hydrogen from sea water are nuclear power, hydroelectric power, geothermal energy, and ocean thermal energy. Although geothermal resources exist in Japan, Taiwan, and the volcanic Pacific islands, and although untapped hydroelectric power exists in the Philippines, Indonesia, Thailand, and Korea, the magnitude of these energy resources is small compared to the requirements of the synthetic fuel industry. The most reasonable alternate energy source may therefore be ocean thermal energy conversion (OTEC). This source will probably develop in the form of floating or "grazing" OTEC plants that manufacture, store, and distribute ammonia, hydrogen, methanol, and other forms of synthetic fuel.

Though OTEC will very likely be a major source of world energy in the next few decades, its implications for the oceans as a commons and for UNCLOS have not as yet been part of international debate at the Law of the Sea negotiations or elsewhere.

OTEC: Concepts and Implications

OTEC warrants extensive review in that readers may not realize its significance as a major energy issue in the next several decades. The concept of obtaining energy from the difference of temperature between the surface of the ocean and the deep ocean is not new, but dates back at least to Arsène d'Arsonval (1881). During the early 1930s, the noted engineer Georges Claude seriously investigated ocean thermal energy, correctly but prematurely anticipating energy shortages. His brilliant test installation demonstrated the viability of the concept (although it did not produce net power). His calculations demonstrated that the energy produced would not be competitive with oil at ten cents a barrel.

Ocean energy was reconsidered in the early 1970s by a number of investigators who anticipated that OTEC might prove economically feasible because of rapidly rising oil prices. The investigators were aware that the necessary installations would be large and capital-intensive, and they also expected that the installation and operation of the cold water pipe (a vertical pipe of large diameter, some 800 meters long) and the biofouling of heat exchangers would pose difficult technical problems. Initial calculations showing that OTEC would be economically competitive were doubted. But in August of 1979 a pilot plant called Mini-OTEC, built by the Lockheed Corporation, Alfa Laval, the Dillingham Corporation, and the State of Hawaii, produced the first net power from ocean thermal energy (more than 10 kilowatts out of 40 kilowatts gross). The test also demonstrated that the engineering problems of the cold water pipe were manageable and that biofouling was controllable.

Since then at least ten independent investigators (Applied Physics Laboratory, Johns Hopkins, The Rand Corporation, Science Applications Incorporated, the Hawaii Natural Energy Institute, Lockheed, TRW, Westinghouse, General Electric, and Toshiba) have concluded that electricity produced from ocean thermal energy will be cost-competitive with electricity produced by coal or by nuclear power. OTEC's initial implications alone are staggering.

An economically viable OTEC would be a renewable resource of tremendous value. *The annual production of energy from this tropical source can potentially be well in excess of 300 quads of energy per year (1 quad is 1×10^{15} BTU) — that is, in excess of the current world consumption of energy.* Considering the magnitude of the resource and the successful development efforts to date, OTEC proponents are understandably frustrated by arguments that OTEC can only be produced where not needed — in the tropical oceans. But oil is also obtained in places remote from its users — the Middle East, or Alaska's North Slope, or the marine environment of continental shelves. Therefore, oil and OTEC transportation issues are comparatively similar.

Oil is at least as remote as OTEC and in addition is accessible to most nations only if it passes successfully through politically sensitive and vulnerable choke points (the several straits and canals). Military, political, and economic uncertainties abound. However, the liabilities of oil transport have been discounted because of the incalculable capital investment already made in its transportation, processing, and use; technology and world society have been tailored to an oil-based energy economy. Because oil is continuously depleted, the capital investment required to maintain an oil supply will continue to leave little, if any, capital for development of substitute systems. It is natural, then, that research and development should remain focused on an oil-based economy — synthetic fuels derived from coal and shale, more natural gas, and further exploitation of ocean oil. This capital constraint will place a brake on OTEC's development. Though the potential is revolutionary, the development of ocean thermal energy will, by virtue of restricted investment, be evolutionary. *The evolution—from an energy economy based on dwindling energy resources to one based on renewable resources—should provide a unique opportunity for the world's island communities to serve as models for the transition.*

The pace of this transition will depend on the economic and cultural needs of the communities in the OTEC belt, the state of the world energy situation, and the status of the oceans as a commons. Considering these factors, a scenario exists for OTEC to meet the energy needs of the Pacific islands in the late 1980s or early 1990s. OTEC could contribute to the needs of the entire Pacific Basin before the turn of the century and be a major source of world energy in the first decade of the twenty-first century.

The nations and communities of the OTEC belt (plus or minus twenty degrees latitude) are not homogeneous. (See Figure 3.) Many are Third World states: Brazil, Ecuador, and Peru; the African states of Liberia, Benin, Ivory Coast, and Cameroon; and farther east, Sri Lanka and India. Mexico and nations in the Isthmus of Panama are continental states that have rich thermal resources in their 200-mile exclusive zones. The major archipelagos with access to such waters are Indonesia, the Philippines, and Japan.

Lyle Dunbar of Science Applications Incorporated has identified 98 nations and territories having access to the resource. Of these, 3 are developed nations (United States, Japan, and Australia), 29 are territories of developed nations, 3 are socialist (Cuba, China, and Vietnam), and 63 are free-market developing nations.

Some of the smaller nations or territories, such as the sparsely populated Pacific islands known as Oceania, are separated by thousands of miles; their total energy needs are miniscule by world standards and met almost entirely by oil imports. A few of the island domains are both politically and economically independent. Fiji, Tonga, Western Samoa, Vanuatu, the Kiribati (Gilberts), and the Solomons have recently acquired independence. Per-capita income is low; the primary sources of hard currency are fishing, canning, copra, and tourism. Energy is furnished by diesel or gasoline generators. Energy uses include imported propane and na-

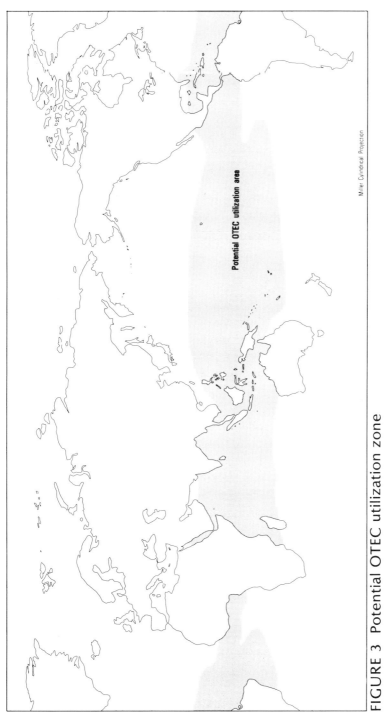

Miller Cylindrical Projection

Potential OTEC utilization area

FIGURE 3 Potential OTEC utilization zone

tural gas for domestic and commercial purposes. Fuel costs in these remote islands are 30–50 percent higher than costs on the continent. Major cost factors are transportation and storage.

Most of the islands have a trustee status or are economically dependent upon more affluent, industrialized states. The Cook Islands are dependent upon New Zealand ($4,500 per-capita GNP); the Marshall and Caroline Islands have a new relationship with the United States ($9,000 per-capita GNP); and Nauru has a trust relationship with Australia ($7,000 per-capita GNP). The remaining islands are possessions, territories, or metropolitan districts of continental or island states. These include Easter Island (Chile, $1,000 per-capita GNP); the Galápagos (Ecuador, $800 per-capita GNP); French Polynesia (France, $7,500 per-capita GNP); Okinawa (Japan, $7,000 per-capita GNP); the Commonwealth of the Marianas, Guam, Wake, Howland, Baker, the Palmyra Islands, and American Samoa—and the Hawaiian archipelago (United States, $9,000 per-capita GNP). The socialist countries are, for historical reasons, underrepresented in access to ocean thermal resources.

Energy needs are small for the Pacific island communities compared to the entire Pacific region and the world, with the exceptions of Hawaii, Okinawa, and Guam. Thus OTEC for domestic use is close to irrelevant for the smaller island communities. Even if a sovereign island nation were given an OTEC electrical plant, the energy would be in a form impossible to distribute among the many small, separate island communities. Table 1 lists the maximum probable indigenous energy consumption for the island domains and the total OTEC resources available to these communities. This table is the subjective estimate of the author and is based on a demand of from one-fourth to two-thirds the per-capita, per-year consumption of the United States. The specific choice was based on estimates of the rate of growth of each economy and its needs. Except for Hawaii, the electrical needs of Oceania are below the threshold of economically viable OTEC projects (100 to 300 Megawatts). The table also contains extremely rough estimates of the magnitude of the ther-

Table 1

Maximum Probable Indigenous Annual Energy Consumption and
Probable Resource Availability
(in quads)

	Energy Consumption	OTEC Availability
Pitcairn Island	0.00002	1.0
Wake Island	0.0002	2.5
Commonwealth of Marianas	0.002	6.0
Guam	0.03	2.0
Fiji	0.1	5.0
Hawaii	0.3	12.0
Oceania (less Hawaii)	0.5	300.0 +
Puerto Rico	1.0	1.0
West Indies (including Puerto Rico)	5.0	50.0
Philippines	6.0	8.0
Indonesia	20.0	25.0
Japan	35.0	10.0
Continental USA	80.0	1.0
USA (including Trust Territories)	80.0	80.0 +

mal energy resources. *Except for the major Western Pacific archipelagos (Indonesia and the Philippines) the energy needs and OTEC energy availability are inversely related.* OTEC energy must therefore be generated in a form that is exportable, from the regions in which it can be generated to the regions where it will be consumed.

OTEC: A Source of Carbon-Free Energy

The fundamental virtue of OTEC is that it can generate hydrogen on the high seas without producing carbon or carbon dioxide as a waste product. This is because the electricity generated by OTEC can be employed for electrolytic dissociation of water molecules into hydrogen and oxygen. The comparative significance of this fact can be appreciated by examining the major problems with current energy use. The three major concerns are: (1) the increase in the atmospheric concentration of CO_2 (carbon dioxide) and other pollutants such as SO_2 (sulfur dioxide); (2) the "plutonium overhang" associated with nuclear power; and (3) the need for hydrogen derived from the water molecule to convert coal into an acceptable synthetic fuel, or to hydrogenate oil in order to make it a more efficient fuel.

The first of these problems seems politically and economically insoluble. Although scientists are never sure, climatologists are "relatively sure" that the buildup in atmospheric CO_2 will result in major climatic changes that will be most detrimental to the Northern Temperate Zone. They assert that these changes will occur early in the twenty-first century, based on the current consumption levels of fossil fuels. Within this time constraint, there appears no significant way to reduce the use of hydrocarbons as the major automotive fuel. However, every effort should be made to reduce the amount of CO_2 that is thereby generated.

A major step in this direction would be a shift from oil- and coal-fired steam turbines, gas turbines, diesel electric, and gasoline electric generation to the hydrogen-fueled or ammonia-fueled fuel cell. OTEC can be a source of carbon-free fuel for such fuel cells.

The fuel cell for prime electrical power is a recent technological development that is still in the pilot plant demonstration stage (albeit successful). Fuel cells are far more efficient in the conversion of chemical fuels to electrical energy than conventional power plant systems. This efficiency is not automatically achieved since fuel cells are most effective when using hydrogen-rich fuels and fuels that are clean. Fossil fuels do not automatically qualify as fuel cell fuels, and energy is required to make them usable. The energy expended for cleanup and conversion, and the pollutants placed in the atmosphere by this process, may vitiate the advantages of the fuel cell. Even so, the fuel cell for peak load and prime electrical power will probably play a substantial role in public utility power generation because it is clean, attractive, and safe (e.g., it can be located in the center of an urban complex without threat of local pollution or nuclear release). As a consequence, much more expensive fuels (higher cost per BTU) can be economically employed in fuel cell systems. For example, an ammonia fuel cell costing three to four times the price of fossil fuel would, other things being equal, be competitive with conventional steam or gas turbines. OTEC-generated ammonia would clearly qualify as such a fuel and would not generate CO_2 in the process.

Hydrogen-rich fuels may also be obtained from gas and oil. Similarly, other methods of power generation can be employed to produce carbon-free fuels. These other methods include the electrolytic decomposition of water using hydroelectric, geothermal, or nuclear power, or biomass-produced alcohols for which the net CO_2 balance is essentially zero. However, these methods will be competitive with OTEC only in the short run because of (1) the limited quantity of hydroelectric and geothermal resources, (2) public desire to limit the growth of nuclear power, and (3) the fact that the gasohol production process is and for some time will be marginally productive of net energy. Hence the demand for hydrogen for fuel cell consumption should provide a ready market for OTEC hydrogen and hydrogen products.

OTEC and Synthetic Fuel

A more recently recognized use for OTEC is in the manufacture of *synthetic fuel*. Even technologists are sometimes surprised to learn that the major barrier to the production of synthetic fuel from coal is the deficiency of hydrogen. The mean value for the molecular ratio of hydrogen to carbon in bituminous coal is about 0.8. The mean hydrogen/carbon ratio for premium fuels is about 2.0. The conversion of coal to synthetic fuel thus requires the addition of hydrogen or the elimination of carbon. A simple calculation demonstrates that the choice of alternatives has an enormous impact on the world energy picture.

At the present time it requires two quads of coal to make one quad of synfuel. The extra quad must be converted to coke or carbon dioxide or a combination of both. If OTEC hydrogen were employed for the enrichment of coal, then only slightly more than one quad of coal (1.1 quads) would be required for each quad of synfuel. Similar though less dramatic ratios exist for the conversion of "coil" (a liquid combination of coal slurry and crude oil) into synthetic fuel, or the conversion of heavy crudes into light crudes.

Recently William H. Avery of the Applied Physics Laboratory has developed a process for the production of methanol from OTEC hydrogen, OTEC oxygen, and coke.[7] In essence his process envisions the pyrolysis (heating in the absence of oxygen) of coal at the mouth of the mine to extract all available hydrocarbons (methane, coal oil, and ammonia). The relatively pure coke that is the residue of the process can be transported to an OTEC site and burned in the presence of OTEC oxygen to produce carbon monoxide and energy in the form of heat. The heat can be converted to electricity for use in the additional dissociation of water into oxygen and hydrogen. The carbon monoxide can be combined with OTEC hydrogen (with the aid of a catalyst) to produce methanol. Avery's estimate of cost vs. return is that, depending on the current market value of methanol, the return realized on the investment will range from 18 to 94 percent per year.[8]

Other factors favoring the production of synfuels from coal and OTEC hydrogen are the economies of scale associated with sea-based siting of production plants, the availability of water for dissociation (roughly 100,000 acre-feet of water per year for each 5 quads of synthetic fuel), and the use of water as a process fluid. The Avery study includes a number of factors which suggest that OTEC-coal synfuels could be the most competitive of the currently proposed synfuels. These factors include: (1) the low electricity cost at the OTEC plant site, (2) the increasing efficiency of electrolytic processes for dissociating hydrogen from water molecules, (3) the proximity of coal to many seaboards, (4) the already developed logistical systems for sea-based transport and distribution of fuels, and (5) the environmental and safety advantages of sea-based installations.

Many will argue that the world ought to bypass the development of hydrocarbon-based synthetic fuels and proceed directly to a hydrogen economy. This might be logically correct, but it would require draconian measures for its implementation. Thus the development of OTEC synfuel will be required because the world is unable to make a rapid leap to a carbon-free energy economy. Such a leap is technologically feasible if ammonia is substituted for hydrocarbon fuels. Ammonia has only about half as many BTU's per pound as gasoline but is a pollution-free fuel that has been used successfully in tractors, automobiles, and other internal combustion equipment. It has been suggested that an oceanic archipelago could become energy self-sufficient. This could be accomplished, for example, with one central OTEC plant (10 kilowatts to 1 Megawatt) employed for producing ammonia. The ammonia, in turn, could be used in fuel cells for electricity and for the powering of automotive equipment.

The pilot operations for these developments are already under way. Tokyo Electric has constructed a 100-kilowatt (net power) OTEC in Nauru. Mitsui-Toshiba is planning the construction of an island OTEC plant for electricity and aquaculture in a Pacific atoll. An American consortium is proposing a grazing 40-Megawatt ammonia plant and half a dozen other consortia are proposing various forms of 10–40 Megawatt electrical energy plants. A pilot project for OTEC synfuels is under serious study and should be under way when this monograph is published. It is not too early, then, to speculate on the probable development process. Four phases can be identified as follows:

1. The development of a series of prototype plants of from 1 to 40 Megawatts. These plants will probably include a grazing ammonia plant, synthetic fuel plants, several electrical power plants, and an aquacultural facility. Both open-cycle and closed-cycle prototypes will probably be developed. Simultaneously, one or more archipelagos will seek energy self-sufficiency by employing ammonia fuel cells and modified ammonia-powered vehicles.

2. The construction of a series of island plants to provide prime electrical power for Honolulu, Puerto Rico, Okinawa, etc., and for island industries such as manganese nodule processing and aluminum production in the Pacific, and petrochemical production in the Caribbean. Prototype develop-

ment plantships (grazing plants) and other plants could also be deployed in the island archipelagos to provide self-sufficiency.

3. The construction of OTEC plants for the manufacture and export of synthetic fuels, utilizing coal and OTEC hydrogen as resources, and the construction of OTEC plants for the manufacture of ammonia to be used in fuel cell power systems for major continental power grids.

4. The ubiquitous use of ammonia in automobiles, the development of hydrogen-powered commercial aircraft, and the transfer of OTEC technology to Third World countries for their use as a major energy source.

OTEC and Ocean Law

Armed with this understanding of OTEC's future we can now explore the probable future of the Law of the Sea as it relates to OTEC. The UNCLOS text is mostly silent on ocean energy except for the 200-mile Exclusive Economic Zone where coastal state sovereignty extends to economic exploitation "such as the production of energy from the water, currents and wind."[9] Initially, when OTEC plants will be providing electricity by cable to shore, UNCLOS will be satisfactory for island coastal states. When grazing OTEC ships become a reality, increasing pressure will be exerted for the development of a regime similar to the regime for seabed minerals. This pressure will come from noncoastal, non-tropical nations seeking the benefits of the oceans' "common heritage," and from coastal states wanting strict production controls on the high seas in order to insure a monopoly over the resource.

Recently it has been argued that the OTEC resource is so plentiful and tropically ubiquitous that an "OTEC-OPEC" is not feasible. This is probably not true. The productivity per unit of capital investment is highly dependent on temperature differential. The Marshall Islands, for example, have in their 200-mile zone a virtual lock on the highest quality ocean thermal water, provided that grazing OTEC plants could be eliminated or limited on the high seas.

In addition, there will be a linkage between OTEC power

and manganese nodule processing, since the waters beneath which nodules rich in metals occur are also rich in thermal energy. Nations like Kiribati have the potential for dominance of the OTEC/nodule resource if the Law of the Sea restricts both OTEC and deep seabed mining in waters beyond national jurisdiction. This is also the case for OTEC/synfuel with regard to Indonesia, the Philippines, and other oil strait nations.

Nuclear Power and the Seas

A discussion of energy futures using ocean thermal energy would be incomplete without including the Pandora alternative—nuclear power. Our focus will be on the use of the oceans for disposal of wastes, but the most important problem may be the use of the oceans for the siting of nuclear power plants.

The Westinghouse Corporation has completed the design and has attained the sophisticated capability to construct floating plants in an artificial embayment on the continental shelf. A safety feature common to these plants and to military nuclear submarines is that, in the event of reactor catastrophe, the power plants can be jettisoned safely in the ocean without the possibility of a runaway reaction.

Although the Westinghouse plants are designed to carry electricity to shore, floating nuclear plants can be used to manufacture hydrogen or ammonia. Thus this source of energy is exactly equivalent to OTEC energy in the production of ammonia or synfuel. Floating nuclear plants can, of course, be deployed around the world and are not confined to the tropics. Curiously, the UNCLOS treaty has even less to say about nuclear-powered facilities than ocean thermal energy. Presumably, nuclear power for energy is subject to the sovereign rights of the coastal states. However, a nuclear-powered, ammonia-producing plantship apparently could transit economic zones so long as the power is to be used solely for propulsion *during the transit*. It is highly unlikely that a legal regime could be devised that would prevent the operation of nuclear energy plantships on the high seas.

Whether sea-based nuclear power or OTEC becomes the dominant user of the sea for production of energy depends upon the availability of capital to developed and developing states, the legal regimes adopted for the deployment of each form of power, and world attitudes toward nuclear power. Regardless of the relative developments in OTEC and nuclear power, the problems of nuclear waste storage and disposal will be present as long as nuclear power is in use. Because the problems are complex there is a great deal of public misunderstanding of *waste storage and waste disposal.*

The need for *storage* arises from the problem known as "plutonium overhang." As fuel rods employed in nuclear reactors are "spent" they can be reprocessed to recover uranium and other nuclides. The plutonium that is diffused through the rods will be recovered and concentrated in quantities in excess of any industrial needs. Thus, a store of plutonium will accumulate that is sufficiently close to weapons grade to be useful in making crude nuclear weapons of critical mass. This poses a serious security problem.

Storage and security problems associated with plutonium that is recovered from spent fuel rods are far more difficult than the same problems associated with *unprocessed* spent rods. Hence, at present, most of these rods are simply stored in "swimming pools" within the reactor compound. As the rods accumulate, some new storage facilities will be required. Nearly every study of the problem concludes that the best storage and security could be achieved on remote ocean islands. However, the decision to employ an island for this purpose is presumably the prerogative of the nation that owns the island. This raises complex political issues that cannot be resolved without an international agreement.

The problem of waste *disposal* is of even greater international concern. Most studies of waste disposal conclude that one of the most environmentally safe and secure places for storage would be suitably designed canisters embedded in the sediments over a benign tectonic plate (the Pacific plate is closest to ideal). Many nations hold that less stringent precautions are adequate, although they agree on ocean disposal. Their persuasion is that water is an excellent shield, diffusion in the deep water column is slow, and dilution of wastes will be adequate. Some of these nations are disposing of nuclear wastes in the oceans at the present time, and (in their view) in accordance with the United Nations treaty on ocean dumping.

The process of dumping raises both environmental and security problems. Given the present state of technology, waste locations that go unrecorded and become unknown even to the disposer are probably more secure than those that are documented. Environmental knowledge is sacrificed for the security.

The ocean is an effective commons for nuclear wastes. But the concept of a "commons" implies wide participation in decisions about its use, and world or regional public policy may legislate against continuation of this form of waste disposal. (See Chapter 7 for a more detailed discussion of the "commons" concept as applied to the oceans.)

The Ocean as an Energy Commons

If these ocean energy-development scenarios prove to be correct, then a dramatic reversal in the availability of the oceans as an energy commons will be possible. Unlike coal, oil, oil shale, gas, and uranium, the energy-rich medium of OTEC (hot and cold water) is not now subject to appropriation. Nations may, under the concept of the Exclusive Economic Zone (EEZ), act as though they had sovereign control of the resource through sovereign control of the OTEC platform; but they cannot control grazing plants on the high seas. These will have a resource available to them as great as or greater than the resource available in the EEZs. Thus the economic value of tropical water to coastal states is simply that which derives from proximity.

As in the case of the manganese nodules, the optimum strategy for Third World nations in the Tropical Zone is to help place the ocean thermal energy resource in waters *beyond* their national jurisdiction under some newly created international authority like the Sea-Bed Authority, and to see that production limitations are imposed in the international area. In that event, or in the more likely event that OTEC plants are most economically deployed in close proximity to land, the commons status of ocean energy will be greatly reduced, and the incentives for regional cooperation throughout the Pacific Basin will be enhanced.

Consider the optimum nature of energy flows for an OTEC/synfuel energy regime. (Refer to Figures 2 and 3 to compare OTEC waters with coal and oil sources.) Australian coal would be transported in a northerly direction eastward of the Straits of Malacca, the Sunda shelf, and the Philippine archipelago. The most probable intersection with OTEC waters will occur in the EEZs of the island nations and territories that are members of the South Pacific Forum. Synfuels created there would be most easily transported to the Northwest (Japan, Korea, Taiwan, and the Philippines).

A second optimum energy flow would begin with Alaskan coal (also an abundant resource), which would intersect OTEC waters most directly in Hawaii, the Kiribati, and the Marshalls. Dissemination of the energy products would be predominantly westward to meet the energy deficiency of the Western Pacific region, but a significant fraction of the products would be vectored to the west coast of the North American continent.

A third pattern of energy flow could begin with Indonesian and Malaysian crudes (supplemented by Middle East crudes). These crudes would be transported through the straits areas to intersect OTEC waters in the vicinity of the Marianas, the Carolines, the Philippines, the Conins, and the Ryukyus. Hydrogen-enriched fuels would then become available for dissemination to ASEAN nations and other nations on the East Asian continent.

The potentials and the problems of such energy flows, and their implications for the future of the Pacific Community, have been well analyzed by Dr. Frances Lai of the National University of Singapore:

> The diversity of perspectives, the fragmentation of market structure and the predominance of concerns for national interest . . . seem to present a rather pessimistic prospect for

regional cooperation. But this is not necessarily so. ASEAN itself demonstrated the possibility of cooperation among diverse interests. Yet, because of their own experience, ASEAN countries are hesitant about the viability of the Pacific Community concept which encompasses a much greater geographical area with many more diverse cultures and economies.

It is true that there has been increasing economic interdependence among the Pacific nations through trade, but does this alone warrant an institutionalized forum? What are the specific interests and roles of the developed nations, especially Japan and the United States, in a Pacific Community? In recent international dialogues which explored the concept of Pacific Basin cooperation, the supposedly reluctant ASEAN participants seemed quite ready to suggest regional issues such as anti-protectionism, adjustment of north-south relations and stabilization of export earnings of the developing countries, as plausible topics for a Pacific Community forum of cooperation. Yet, they are skeptical about the responses they may get from the more developed countries. Participants from countries such as Japan usually verbalize their idealistic goals in illusive terms. Will these countries be more "cooperative" in a Pacific Community than they have been in bilateral negotiation? What concrete programs of cooperation would they propose? ASEAN feels as if it is participating in a one-sided dialogue. No wonder the ASEAN countries have been showing signs of impatience for a decision from Japan over the kind of organization or program it envisions.

ASEAN has deliberately avoided politics and security issues in their declaration of purpose and solidarity, but it is a known fact that it was political and diplomatic successes that made ASEAN viable. Now, Japan, the main advocate of the Pacific Community Concept, likewise has been avoiding the political and security issues of Pacific Basin cooperation. Is there enough urgency in today's economic issues that would make such a Pacific Community forum necessary and viable?

From our discussion of the energy and oil situation in ASEAN and from a general understanding of the energy future of the Pacific Basin, . . . it seems that the energy needs of the region is one issue that may warrant such urgency. The need for energy is shared by all countries, either for consumption or for foreign exchange and domestic economic development. The impact of rapidly rising oil prices is threatening many nations. If regional stability is the ultimate goal of the Pacific Basin Cooperation Concept, cooperation in the use and management of energy resources would be one of the most crucial areas for joint efforts. In a short term perspective, an effective emergency oil-sharing scheme and crude stockpile would likely benefit all countries in the Pacific and help to buffer them from the drastic effects of oil price/ supply fluctuations. In a long term perspective, joint development of alternative energy would be an ideal forum for genuine exchanges and cooperation. In view of the trend in UNCLOS III of maximizing national interst . . . , alternative energy, such as OTEC, using resources from the ocean commons outside of any national claims, would facilitate cooperation without being unnecessarily entangled in problems of overlapping jurisdiction.

Here we are proposing, in a nutshell, two possible approaches to the evolution of a viable Pacific Basin Cooperation framework. One is the pragmatic approach, whereby interests of potential members are identified and concrete steps are planned to eliminate conflicts and to maximize each other's interests through collective arrangements. Another approach may be called the idealist approach whereby basically non-conflictual common interests are identified and are used as the focus of a forum where people in the region can exchange their ideas and get to know and work with each other under a common identity of a Pacific Community. It is hoped that such a common identity, like that of the EEC or ASEAN, would be catalytic to an eventual trust and greater cooperation in more delicate matters. It is in this latter approach that ASEAN expects more initiatives from the developed countries which have both the technology and financial means.[10]

3
Mineral Futures of the Oceans

Currently, the mineral resources of the Pacific region are derived almost exclusively from land-based sources. Unlike the energy flows, hard minerals are much less dependent on the passage through straits. With a few exceptions, only the major industrialized nations are associated with the production of the major hard minerals used in the Pacific Basin. The bulk of the iron ores used comes from Tasmania. Pacific aluminum comes from Australia, titanium from the USSR, tin from Indonesia, copper from Chile and Australia, and nickel from Canada. A non-Pacific country, Zaire, is the major source of manganese and nickel.

Although there is some inherent dependence on the integrity of the Panama Canal, sources of nearly every major mineral located on land are found in some country on the Pacific rim. However, current estimates suggest that there will be significant depletion of these high grade hard minerals — particularly copper, nickel, cobalt, and manganese — by the turn of the century. (Titanium is already restricted on the world market by the USSR.) This is why the mineral potential of the manganese nodules on the deep seabed has attracted world attention. The ubiquity of the nodules, the rate of accretion (in excess of world consumption of the accreting minerals), and the great mineral concentrations suggest that the mining and processing of these minerals should be commercially feasible today. Although manganese nodules are found throughout the world's oceans the currently published results of exploration suggest that nodules richest in cobalt, copper, and nickel occur in an area associated with the Clarion-Clipperton fracture zone. This area lies between

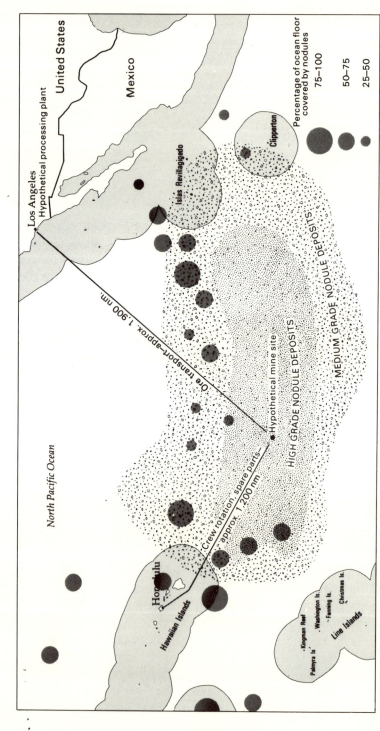

FIGURE 4 North Pacific manganese nodule zone

Hawaii and the Kiribati on the west and Mexico on the east. But manganese nodule crusts (see Figure 4) and pavements rich in titanium and cobalt are associated with volcanic island chains such as the Marianas and the Hawaiian archipelago.

The Non-Law of Seabed Mining

The capital-intensive technology of floating platforms, of dynamic positioning, of sea-generated energy, of deep sea drilling, etc., will find ready application in the mining and processing of manganese nodules. There is fairly uniform agreement that this mining will not take place until an acceptable international regime is in place. The last and still unresolved issue of UNCLOS relates to the details surrounding this regime.

Maltese Ambassador Arvid Pardo's original United Nations resolution, which set off the current UNCLOS negotiations in the early 1970s, declared the resources of the ocean to be "the common heritage of mankind." This has been interpreted by distinguished jurists of the developing world as vesting title to the manganese nodules of the deep seabed in the world community of peoples and as meaning, therefore, that the United Nations is the only agent which can allocate these resources.

Equally distinguished jurists in the industrialized democracies, however, take the position that no property right has been vested (i.e., that the nodules are *res nullius*), and that the oceans' resources are therefore available for exploitation by industrial entrepreneurs whose duty to the common heritage is limited to the payment of royalties. Faced with these diametrically opposing views, the United Nations Conference has been attempting to formulate a legal regime for mining the deep seabed.

Negotiations to date have produced a two-tier system which provides for a United Nations Authority with regulatory powers over mining ventures that may be engaged in either by independent miners or by a United Nations Enterprise. Joint ventures of private entrepreneurs and the Enterprise are also permissible.

Within this framework, three competing interests can be identified: those of the developing nations that do not possess land-based mineral resources; those of the nations, developed and underdeveloped, that are land-based producers; and those of the developed nations that do not have significant land-based minerals. The first interest desires a highly effective United Nations Enterprise with full access to the world's technology so that it can dominate the world market. Capitalist enterprises would be tolerated only in the transition from the old to the new economic order. The second interest desires a carefully controlled United Nations cartel in which seabed resources would meet only shortages, in order to protect the interests of land-based producers. The third interest desires a regime in which capital-intensive, competitive, sea-based private enterprise can compete with land-based producers.

The struggle to shape a legal regime that accommodates these mutually exclusive interests has resulted in one of the most technically complicated international treaties ever. It contains, for example, mathematical formulas based on exponential relationships; it may be the first treaty to incorporate a "regression formula" in the body of the text. The current treaty draft most closely represents the second interest, that of nations favoring a restrictive international cartel.

Some form of this arrangement will prove acceptable to the companies of the industrialized democracies that are not producers, or major exporters, of land-based minerals (United States, Japan, Germany), provided they have a seat in the club. National legislation, pending for some time in the United States Congress, has finally become law; it provides unilateral protection for United States miners provided that seabed operations do not commence prior to 1988. But this legislation will be superseded by the treaty when and if it comes into force. Such legislation will virtually ensure that a U.S. company or companies will be part of the world consortium. Other nations have followed suit with unilateral legislation, and efforts are now under way among the industrialized nations to harmonize their somewhat differing legislative measures.

The extremely large investment required for ocean mining or for the extraction of oil from the seabed makes it highly unlikely that any entrepreneur will engage in this activity without the protection of some sovereign state or conformance with international law. Although clandestine or illegal exploitation of the mineral resources of the seabed is highly unlikely, clandestine and illegal *explorations* are probably common practice. A large amount of unreported exploratory drilling has probably taken place, and will continue to take place on U.S. continental shelves. This is also true of offshore waters in East Asia and Southeast Asia. Researchers who listen in on ocean channels on a regular basis know that deliberately generated seismic and acoustic signals are always present, although it is difficult to determine the location of the source. It would be naive to believe that all such activity takes place in conformance with international and municipal laws and regulations.

Whatever the legalities, there is no doubt that major economic entities can acquire information about the location and quality of oil or mineral resources of the oceans, and that this information provides them an advantage in negotiating with sovereignties and authorities.

On a time scale that is at this date quite uncertain, the recovery of mineral resources from the ocean will shift from manganese nodules to the recovery of metal sulfides associated with geothermal vents. The vents are vertical pipes of molten magma that intrude into the oceans in regions where the tectonic plates are separating and fracturing. Fractional distillation of the molten minerals produces a layering and concentration of high grade mineral deposits. Once dormant, these vents should be excellent mine sites.

Surveys conducted by the National Ocean Survey have shown — rather conclusively — that the Clarion-Clipperton fracture zone is a highly promising geophysical structure for the location of these dormant vents. The submarine Alvin, on research dives, has recovered rocks weighing hundreds of pounds having copper content as high as 20 percent. Thus there exist divided opinions as to the most probable scenario—an ordered prospecting, survey, and development of mine sites over twenty to twenty-five years, or a short-term mineral rush.

As fate would have it, the Clarion-Clipperton fracture zone is roughly 200 miles to sea, intersecting with, impinging upon, or skirting the EEZs of the Galápagos, Mexico, the United States, and Canada. It is clear that the present legal regime for manganese nodule processing, which is based on very wide distribution of the resource over a large area, will be inappropriate for management of the vents.

Six Seabed Mining Scenarios

On the initial presumption that the ocean was a commons with unlimited access, manganese nodule mining companies began exploring deep seabed resources some fifteen years ago. The following up-to-date analysis of the policy tangle in which they now find themselves is taken from Kent Keith's paper from the June 1981 Tokyo workshop.

> By 1975, more than 100 companies around the world were involved in some aspect of manganese nodule mining. It is estimated that over $300 million has now been spent on various international consortia to explore the ocean floor, to test mining equipment, and to research processing techniques for a manganese nodule industry. Considering the number of years, the money invested, and the companies interested, it is not hard to understand why many experts expected manganese nodule mining to be a reality by the late 1970s. As we know, of course, the scale-up to commercialization has not yet begun.
>
> While there are technological problems yet to be overcome, the root of the present delay appears to be primarily political. In general, the companies appear to be waiting for a resolution of the deep seabed mining issues at the United Nations Third Conference on the Law of the Sea (UNCLOS III). The United States and West Germany have passed national legislation regarding manganese nodule mining, but this, in and of

itself, has not been sufficient to stimulate the scale-up to commercialization.

Six scenarios can be drawn to focus the issues and stimulate discussion on the prospects for marine mining in the 1980s. These scenarios are:

1. The mining consortia wait until an UNCLOS III treaty is ratified, and then begin mining under the treaty provisions.

2. While awaiting ratification of an UNCLOS III treaty, the consortia proceed under unilateral national legislation or a reciprocating States regime which will be superseded by the treaty when it comes into force.

3. The governments of a number of States decline to ratify the UNCLOS III treaty, and mining begins under unilateral legislation or a reciprocating States regime.

4. The mining consortia enter into agreements with coastal States and mine nodules, metallic crusts, or metallic brines within the 200-mile Exclusive Economic Zones of those States.

5. The existing mining consortia disband, and conduct no further activities in the 1980s.

6. All or several of the above.

Scenario #1: Waiting for the Treaty

Waiting for the treaty may be the scenario adopted by those companies which are multinational or transnational in their activities. Companies which are now doing business in the Third World may want to stay on good terms with the less developed States at UNCLOS III. The existing investments and enterprises of these multinational companies may simply be too great to set at risk over deep-sea mining. One thing they may not wish to set at risk is oil. It is significant that one of the three owners of Ocean Mining Associates is Sun Oil Company; two of the owners of Ocean Minerals Company are Standard Oil of Indiana (Amoco) and Royal Dutch Shell; and British Petroleum has a 53 percent interest in Standard Oil of Ohio (Sohio), which has recently taken over Kennecott Copper. The oil industry is bigger than marine mining is likely to be for many decades. This perspective may be persuasive for some corporate leaders.

Waiting for the treaty may also be the policy of developed States dependent on less-developed States for their current supply of strategic metals. The developed State may be interested in developing marine minerals as a new source of supply, but not be capable of marine mining for many years. In the meantime, it could not afford to be cut off by land-based suppliers. By supporting the treaty, the developed State signals that it will only begin mining under treaty terms acceptable to the less-developed States. Presumably, there would thus be little reason for the less-developed States to cut off supplies to the developed State in the scale-up period before mining begins.

Waiting for the treaty may also be the position of the financial communities of developed States. National unilateral legislation may provide for the establishment of claims, and a reciprocating States regime would resolve conflicts between the companies of different States. While some security is thereby provided, the question hovers in the background: If an UNCLOS III treaty is ratified, will the International Sea-Bed Authority recognize the claims established under a reciprocating States regime? If not what is the point of proceeding? Until the Authority accepts the claim, the investment risk may be too high. Security of tenure depends on a successful transition from the validation of claims by reciprocating States to validation by the Authority. Since that transition cannot be assured, the financiers may prefer to wait.

One disadvantage of waiting for the treaty is that the treaty may be unfavorable to the mining companies. In both public and private statements, many members of the consortia have been critical of the Draft Convention of the Law of the Sea currently being discussed at UNCLOS III. In general, those States with the technology and capital available to develop deep ocean mining technology are those States with free enterprise or modified capitalist systems. In those systems, companies generally compete with each other, while the government plays the role of referee or guide. The proposed international regime for deep seabed mining under an UNCLOS III treaty is alien to these companies. Under proposed treaty provisions, a company would have to contribute a share of profits to develop "the common heritage" for the benefit of mankind, especially the developing States; it would have to live within certain quotas, which would give it less flexibility in responding to the market; it would have to transfer technology which may be its prime asset in market competition; and most unusual of all, if would have to compete with an Enterprise which is the organ of its regulator. The International Sea-Bed Authority will set the rules, and may set them to the advantage of one of the competitors, the Enterprise.

Another disadvantage of waiting is that waiting does not assure an UNCLOS III treaty. There may never be one, or it may have too few parties to enter into force, or too few parties to be effective after entering into force. Even with success assured, the wait could be very long. International experience with treaty-making is not encouraging. One commentator suggests that 80 parties will be necessary for an UNCLOS III treaty to be a success. However, the multilateral treaties which entered into force from 1947–1971 averaged only 30–48 parties. Even large, relatively non-controversial treaty-making efforts have not resulted in a large number of ratifying parties. For example, the 1968–69 Vienna Conference on the Law of Treaties was attended by 110 States; the final text was accepted by 79, and it was signed by only 47. By 1980, ten years later, only 33 States had ratified or acceded to the treaty, two short of the number needed to enter into force.

Fifteen ocean-related treaties which came into force after 1946 were still in force by 1979. Most of these treaties were narrowly focused and relatively unimportant. Only three achieved more than 80 parties — the IMCO Convention, the International Convention for the Safety of Life at Sea, and the International Convention on Loadlines. The proposed UNCLOS III treaty, of course, is far broader in scope than these treaties. A more meaningful comparison is with the four 1958 Geneva Conventions and Optional Protocol. States could sign the individual conventions; only 14 signed all five. Since all five together are equivalent to the UNCLOS III treaty, there is some doubt as to whether UNCLOS III will attract the 36–50 parties to enter into force or the 80 to become a success.

If the treaty does enter into force, it could take many years to do so. It took an average of six years for the four Geneva Conventions to enter into force. The Territorial Sea Convention was signed by forty three States, less than half of those at the Conference. Only half of those forty three have ratified the treaty in the twenty years since then. The least controversial Convention, the Convention on the High Seas, took thirteen years to obtain fifty parties.

Achieving agreement on the proposed UNCLOS III treaty

is a monumental task, unparalleled in the number of States involved and the breadth of issues included. It has taken seven years so far, and seeing it through ratification could take another decade or more. The disadvantage of waiting for the treaty is thus that the wait will be long and the outcome is not certain.

Scenario #2: Unilateral Action or a Reciprocating States Regime While Waiting for the Treaty

The desire to preserve industry momentum may lead to commercialization and even mining under unilateral legislation or a reciprocating States regime while awaiting the ratification of an UNCLOS III treaty. The Deep Seabed Hard Mineral Resources Act which was enacted on June 28, 1980 in the United States and the Act on Interim Regulation of Deep Seabed Mining which was promulgated on August 16, 1980 in the Federal Republic of Germany both provide that commercial mining may begin before the ratification of an UNCLOS III treaty. However, both laws provide that commercial mining shall not be permitted before January 1, 1988. This gives UNCLOS III seven years to obtain ratification of a treaty before U.S. or West German companies begin commercial operations. Each law allows the creation of a reciprocating States regime while the treaty moves toward ratification.

This scenario provides a fallback position in the event a treaty does not enter into force. This scenario would also be attractive if a company could be assured of mining its chosen sites for five to ten years before a treaty takes effect. That period of time could be sufficient to recover capital costs and obtain a return on investment. However, while it could take ten years for the treaty to be ratified, industry needs seven or eight years just to scale up for commercial operations. Adding ten years for commercial activity means seventeen to eighteen years, and the ratification of the treaty may not take that long.

Another attractive aspect of moving ahead before an UNCLOS III treaty enters into force is the fact that a reciprocating States regime could serve as a model for the Authority. Permit procedures, conflict resolution, and a range of multilateral administrative agreements would be in operation as part of a reciprocating States regime. Their effectiveness will be influential, and the established system could be adopted in whole or in part by the Authority. This could give developed States a role in shaping a regime which is suitable to them.

The disadvantage of this approach is that it does not eliminate the risk that the Authority which comes into existence will not recognize the claims established under the reciprocating States regime. This risk could be allayed by national legislation providing insurance or compensation, an approach which was rejected by the Congress in passing the U.S. legislation and the Bundestag in passing the West German legislation.

Scenario #3: Unilateral Action by, or a Reciprocating States Regime Among Those not Party to the Treaty

A number of states may decline to ratify the treaty. Unilateral action by the States with mining technology might lead quickly to a multilateral treaty or reciprocating States regime. A multilateral treaty among those nations capable and interested in manganese nodule mining would be consistent with the pattern of international law over the past centuries. Those nations with the ability to conduct deep ocean mining would negotiate a treaty to protect their own claims. A reciprocating States regime might involve only a handful of countries — U.S., Germany, Britain, Japan, France, the Netherlands, Belgium, and Italy. But since these are the major countries whose governments and companies are involved in deep ocean mining development, an agreement among these States could establish a workable international regime. This agreement could be reached after each government has declined to ratify an UNCLOS III treaty. States may oppose specific treaty terms, and may also believe that much of what is good in the treaty has already become accepted and may even be customary international law. The acceptance of an Exclusive Economic Zone is an example of a major new concept which benefits many coastal States and is not likely to be challenged even if it is not specifically ratified in the form of an UNCLOS III treaty.

No doubt, technologically advanced nations have something to lose, either ideologically or practically, by rejecting the treaty. Presumably, they would not be at the bargaining table unless they felt there was something to gain. However, technologically advanced nations are vulnerable to a shut down of their entire economies if critical metals are not available. The U.S., for example, is dependent upon imports for overwhelming percentages of many critical metals. It is no surprise that one of the most active consortia today is Ocean Mining Associates, which is partly owned by U.S. Steel. U.S. Steel needs manganese as a scavenger and alloy in steel production. The U.S. imports 98 percent of its manganese. While the total amount needed is not large and might be supplied by a single ocean mining operation, the metal is critical to U.S. industry.

This scenario may be adopted by developed States which are willing to risk conflict in order to obtain a stable source of supply of critical metals. The disadvantages are uncertain. The prospects for a reciprocating States regime which has rejected the treaty are clouded by the fact that a treaty could be ratified by the less-developed States and be considered by them to be in full force and effect. The Authority would be brought into existence, and would be in direct conflict with the activities of a reciprocating States regime which consisted of States rejecting the treaty. Should a situation such as this come to pass, the Authority would be obliged to assert its regulatory control, since it would otherwise have no one to regulate and no profits to share as the common heritage of mankind. In response, the governments of the reciprocating States regime would be obliged to protect the interests of their nationals. At best, this conflict could lead to the negotiating table for more years of discussion. The rejection of the treaty and establishment of a reciprocating States regime could thus give those reciprocating States a better bargaining position in achieving a final resolution many years further down the road. However, the conflict could also lead to retaliation, such as boycotts, cartel action, the cutting off of land-based supplies, and other "economic warfare." At worst, the conflict could lead to incidents of actual warfare. Retaliatory action by less developed States would be modified by the need of some States to continue selling products—including land-based metals—to developed States, or the need of some less developed States to obtain capital from developed States for a variety of projects.

A further disadvantage is that not all States passing unilateral legislation may become part of a reciprocating States regime. Differences in national legislation may preclude reciprocal recognition. This could create confusion and result

in conflicting claims. Also, in the same way that "flags of convenience" have affected marine shipping, "permits of convenience" may affect marine mining. As one commentator
notes, ". . . if nations initiate deep seabed mining under
reasonable regulatory programmes on the basis that such
mining is a freedom of the high seas, there is an inherent risk
that other nations may abuse this freedom." If they do, an in-
clusive reciprocating States regime may not be possible.

*Scenario #4: Marine Mining Within Exclusive
Economic Zones*

The mining consortia with an immediate need for critical
metals may move to exploit the marine minerals within
200-mile Exclusive Economic Zones (EEZs). Within each
EEZ, the mining consortia would not have to wait ten years
for ratification of an UNCLOS III treaty, or take the risk of
operating under a reciprocating States regime which conflicts
with or is superseded by an Authority. The advantage to the
coastal State is that it may be able to negotiate a favorable arrangement to obtain a share of the profits for itself, rather
than sharing the profits among the entire common heritage of
mankind. This would not violate the spirit of the proposed
UNCLOS III treaty, since that treaty would establish exclusive economic zones for purposes such as this.

There are several disadvantages to this approach. First of
all, the richest known deposits of manganese nodules are in
the deepest ocean waters, far beyond most EEZs. Deposits
within the EEZs may not be as valuable. Second, deposits
within 200-mile zones may be in the form of multi-metallic
crusts or metallic brines rather than nodules. Mining these
deposits would require a reworking of the mining technology.
Also there is the simple fact that surveying, sampling, and
analyzing prospective marine mining sites can take many
years. Surveying and sampling in the Clarion-Clipperton fracture zone has been going on for a decade, and companies are
only now finalizing the sites for which they would like to file
mining claims. It would take a number of years to evaluate
the metallic deposits within the EEZs of countries interested
in doing business. Mining in the EEZs may thus be several
years behind the state of the art for deep-sea mining in the
Clarion-Clipperton fracture zone.

Yet three examples indicate the potential of this approach.

First of all, Chile has issued a notice that it will welcome bids for manganese nodule mining within its 200-mile zone around an offshore island known as Juan Fernandez Island. Another area of interest is found within the 200-mile zone around Mexico's Revillagigedo archipelago, 800 km west of the mainland. Perhaps more instructive is the agreement already reached by Preussag Aktiengesellschaft, a German company, to mine metalliferous sediments in the Red Sea. Preussag intends to begin mining this summer backed by Arabian oil money and with the permission of the coastal State. Thus, the first major marine mining operation will in fact be within an EEZ, but it will not be a manganese nodule mining operation.

Scenario #5: The Existing Nodule Mining Consortia Give Up

International mining ventures are often joint ventures established to share the risks and accumulate capital for specific projects. These appear to be two of the major reasons the existing consortia were formed. Much of the attention of the consortia has been focused on security for their investments, in order to obtain capital from the money markets. A single mining operation could require a capital investment of anywhere between $900 million and $1.4 billion in today's dollars, and the mining consortia may not be able to obtain this kind of money without investment banker support. This is not an especially large amount of money, compared to other mining projects. Money may be hard to come by, however, since a treaty could be unfavorable to a return on investment; a reciprocating States regime pending a treaty could end in the non-recognition of the investment by a new Authority; a reciprocating States regime among States not party to the treaty could lead to conflict; and it may not be feasible to rework the mining technology and obtain satisfactory agreements with coastal States for mining in the EEZs. Thus, a sufficient amount of money may not be available in the coming decade under the four scenarios discussed above. If so, the existing consortia may decide to defer action or give up and write off their losses.

Even if money becomes available, the companies involved in these consortia have many economic opportunities outside of marine mining. Other opportunities may have an earlier payback period, and be less risky. In addition to money, the consortia have assigned key personnel from their own staffs and have kept them at work for a number of years. These people are valuable, and along with the money, may be reassigned to more promising and more immediate opportunities. Once reassigned, it is unlikely that all of these personnel would be available again in the near future. A new team would have to be formed, and much of the previous experience could be lost in the process. Companies may be willing to do this, however, in order to make more productive use of their funds and personnel in the interim. While one or two years of start-up time would be added due to the need to assemble and train a new team, this second start would only be made when there was much greater assurance that mining would indeed take place in the very near future.

For the existing consortia, disbanding may not even mean the forfeiture of each company's leadership position. In light of the head start which the existing consortia have over new entrants into the market, a new entrant with major financing could require three or four years to catch up. The existing consortia would have the same period of time to reactivate their teams or form new teams to continue work based on previous company experience.

For the consortia themselves, the disadvantages of giving up is not only loss of experience on the part of their teams, but the fact that they remain vulnerable to price escalation or the cutoff in supply of metals critical for industry in the developed States. Even if individual companies are willing to risk price escalation or a cutoff in supply, it is not clear that governments are. The governments of the U.S., Germany, and Japan, for example, are likely to encourage and promote the development of the marine mining industry by their private sectors in order to support national strategic interests in metals. Which particular company goes forward may not be at issue; it will be in each developed State's interest that at least one of its companies do so.

"Giving up" may not last beyond the eighties. While supplies of land-based ores may still be large, existing mines will become exhausted or uneconomical. The percentage of value metals in the ores has been decreasing, and the amount of land withdrawn into wilderness or unavailable for technical or environmental reasons has also increased. The cost of land-based mining will thus continue to rise. As for new

mines, the record to date in laterite ore processing is not encouraging. In short, marine minerals will eventually be mined
because they will become economically competitive, and are
the only major long-term alternative to today's land-based
mining.

Scenario #6: All or Several of the Above

The strategic interests of States and the activities of their
companies vary sufficiently that none of the above scenarios
may describe what all of the States or consortia will do. For
example, Ocean Management, Inc. is partly owned by INCO
[Ltd.] [International Nickel Corporation] of Canada, which
has a substantial portion of the world's nickel supply. The
Kennecott Copper Group is led by Kennecott, which has a
substantial portion of the U.S. copper market. Both of these
consortia are largely inactive at present. Since they have significant supplies of land-based ores, they can afford to "give
up" for now. They are in a defensive position—if someone
else moves in to mine, they can reactivate to defend their
market positions.

On the other hand, Ocean Mining Associates (OMA) may
move ahead to secure manganese for U.S. Steel. Ocean
Minerals Company (OMCO) may also move ahead. OMCO is
partly owned by Standard Oil of Indiana, whose subsidiary,
Amoco Minerals Company, has embarked upon a broad program of minerals acquisition. OMA and OMCO may push
for a reciprocating States regime pending an UNCLOS III
treaty. If the U.S. declines to become a party to the treaty,
these companies may seek compensation provisions to proceed under unilateral legislation or a reciprocating States
regime composed of States which are not parties to the treaty.

The existing consortia, of course, may split up. Preussag,
for example, is a member of the OMI [Ocean Management,
Inc.] group, but has ventured on its own to mine metalliferous sediments in the Red Sea. Deep Ocean Mining Company
(DOMCO) of Japan, also an OMI member, may wait for a
treaty. The Japanese government announced last year that it
was launching a seven year research program to survey sites, a
program which is consistent with the timetable for a treaty.
Passage of unilateral legislation which would be superseded
by a treaty would allow Japanese companies to participate
in a reciprocating States regime, which could recognize

and establish DOMCO claims while waiting for treaty ratification.[11]

Seabed Mining and the Commons

As a result of the review of the UNCLOS treaty by the Reagan Administration, international speculation has focused on the alternative scenarios described by Keith. Ambassador T.T.B. (Tommy) Koh, president of the Third United Nations Conference on the Law of the Sea, puts it this way:

> A further possible outcome of the United States review might be the conclusion that the United States . . . was not in favour of a treaty, that its national interests were taken care of by State practice and customary international law in so far as deep seabed mining was concerned, and that it would be preferable to persuade its industrial partners . . . Japan, the United Kingdom, Belgium, and France . . . to enact national legislation with reciprocating provisions . . . a "mini-treaty."
>
> If that option became a reality . . . the developing and the socialist countries might proceed to adopt this treaty, and become party to it . . . with the result that . . . under international law there would be . . . a mini-treaty signed . . . by some five industrial States . . . and a maxi-treaty . . . signed by over 100 States. If the developing countries decided to take the matter to the International Court of Justice . . . the Court might rule in favour of the maxi-treaty side holding that the national laws in question were contrary to international law. In that event . . . those who had developed the expensive seabed mining technology involving major economic investments would obtain the kind of legal security which . . . was . . . necessary . . . for risking the venture capital.[12]

In light of these scenarios and predictions we might ask which, if any, fit within the concept of a marine commons. Certainly it is neither desirable nor necessary that a commons be unregulated. Indeed such lack of regulation would insure one kind of "tragedy of the commons."[13] In this instance the tragedy would most probably be the flooding of the world mineral markets and the financial collapse of the investing entrepreneurs. Three elements appear necessary to satisfy the notion of a global commons: (1) guaranteed access to the resource for all duly constituted economic entities, (2) production limitations in response to world need and demand, and (3) suitable principles for the granting of licenses, assessment of royalties, and apportionment of production limitations. Proponents of UNCLOS III would argue that the proposed text is just such an arrangement. Proponents of a reciprocating states regime argue that their kind of mini-treaty would most closely approximate the ideal. In either event the utilization of this resource in any manner will require some acceptable regime to enable investors to risk the huge amounts of capital required for exploitation.

4

Living Resource Futures of the Oceans

The problems that must be resolved in achieving a regulated and equitable commons in the oceans can be seen most clearly in the case of living resources. Although the economic value of these resources does not match the value of the oceans' use for transportation, energy, defense, or (potentially) mineral resources, the social and political importance of satisfying food needs and dietary preferences makes the status of living marine resources a major international issue. The complexities of ocean energy and mineral recovery may prove to be simplistic when compared to the regimes now developing for the living resources of the sea.

The Diversity of Fisheries

Fishing as an international resource as opposed to a local one was not of significance until the invention of salt preservation in the fourteenth century. Since that time there has been a steady world increase in the annual harvest of marine protein, based on the general notion of the ocean as a commons and the assumption that supply would always exceed demand. In Melville's novel *Moby Dick*, an entire essay is devoted to the inexhaustibility of the world's supply of whales. Even when the error of this assumption became apparent, a similar assumption was made about most other ocean life and was believed to be true until the mid-1940s.

Shortly after World War II scientific concern was directed to the possible exhaustibility of the oceans' living resources.

In 1955, Dr. John Ryther of the Woods Hole Oceanographic Institute estimated that the maximum sustainable yield per year of fish protein (caught by conventional means and from conventional resources) was 55 million metric tons. Last year (1981) and for the past several years, the world catch has been in excess of 70 million metric tons. Overfishing on a world-wide basis has been much in the news as a serious international policy issue. Techniques used by Russian and Japanese fleets have demonstrably depressed populations of fish in a number of traditional fishery areas, particularly off the northeast coast of the United States, and have exacerbated fears about the adequacy of the world's fishery resources.

Fish are of course not evenly distributed throughout the ocean. The normal temperature density structure of the ocean is such that the nutrients required to sustain a standing crop of animals sink into the deep water below the photic zone. Only in places of natural upwelling are the deep, nutrient-rich waters returned to the surface, providing food for a rich fishery. These areas of upwelling are found in (1) two belts above and below the equator, (2) the Arctic and Antarctic, and (3) wherever major currents (for example, the Gulf Stream, Kuroshio, Japanese Current, and Humboldt Current) intersect the coastlines. Thus the Grand Banks; the coasts of Chile, Ecuador, and Peru; Taiwan; and the Alaskan archipelago are among the areas most abundant in fish. (See Figure 5.)

Much of the world's seafood is not fish but arthropods, mollusks, and even reptiles. For all these groups the type of species affects the locale of the resource. Sedentary demersal species of shrimps, oysters, clams, crabs, and lobsters stay more or less fixed within a coastal jurisdiction. Pelagic fish such as the various species of tuna (albacore, yellow fin, big eye), the wahoo, the mahi mahi, and the billfish make regular migrations across the ocean, following paths of high nutrient concentration. The anadromous fish such as salmon begin their life in freshwater streams, move out into the open sea, and return unerringly to the stream from whence they came. Strange but valuable creatures such as the oceanic eel spawn

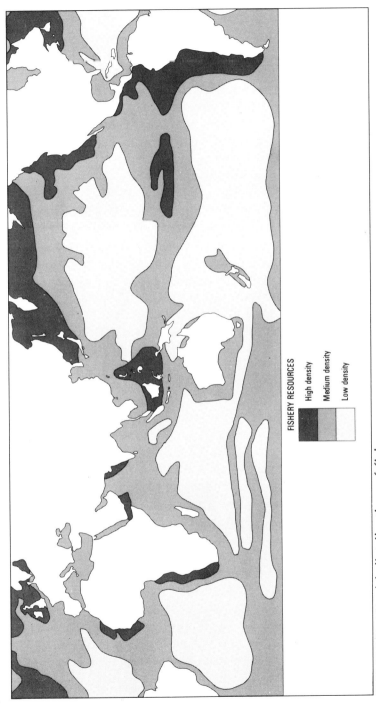

FISHERY RESOURCES

High density

Medium density

Low density

FIGURE 5 World distribution of fishery resources

in unknown regions, spend their lives as elvers in a limited number of coastal waters, and are either impounded in aqua-farms or return to the open sea as they reach maturity.

The Hawaiian green sea turtle begins its life in a United States wildlife bird sanctuary. The few newly hatched turtles that escape from the protected birds enter the waters of Hawaii. Three miles out they are in waters governed by the FCMA (Fisheries Conservation Management Act); for the next two hundred miles they are under the full protection of the endangered species act. They then enter unprotected international waters and are fair game and good eating for any vessel not returning to a U.S. port. In their long migration they swim into and out of international, federal, and state waters under varying degrees of protection (in state waters they may be taken by native Hawaiians for subsistence), until they end up in the soup in Kiribati (the Gilberts).

The greatest impact of changes in the Law of the Sea is felt by traditional fishermen, especially those operating in "distant waters" (as worded in the UNCLOS III treaty). Initially, mutual protection for both the resource and the industry was obtained by regional treaties. These treaties have in general been negotiated for exploitation of fishing resources that require large capital expenditure (tuna, whale). However, only a few nations have fished these resources.

Nonsignatory nations have tacitly agreed not to enter territorial waters. Nonetheless, at times a nation with a quota limit has sold its fishing vessels to a nonsignatory that in turn has harvested the resource in excess of the quota for sale in the ports of the signatory nation.

Within the 200-mile economic zone proposed by the UNCLOS treaty, the harvest of fish is to be managed by the coastal state. Under the treaty terms, the coastal state may reserve to itself that proportion of the maximum sustainable yield of each species that it is capable of harvesting with its fleet of fishing vessels. The excess (if any) must be allocated to other nations with priority to adjacent coastal states and to states that are zone-locked or land-locked by the coastal state having jurisdiction.

U.S. Fishery Management Dilemmas

U.S. fishery problems stem from the diversity of the fishing interests and fisheries. The major distant water fishery is that of the San Diego tuna fleet, whose interest is to pursue the tuna wherever they go. The fleet maintains the right to fish within three miles of any coastal state. For more than two decades the nations of Chile, Ecuador, and Peru have been arresting and fining crews of U.S. tuna boats that venture within their declared 200-mile limits, and the U.S. taxpayer has been paying the fines. The tuna fishermen thus oppose the application of the 200-mile zone to tuna and support such organizations as the Eastern Tropical Tuna Organization, which regulates the catch on a regional basis.

Economically as valuable as the tuna fleet, but with less political clout, is the shrimp fishery. A large portion of its catch is taken in the coastal waters of Brazil and Mexico. The remainder is concentrated in waters of the Gulf. The shrimpmen want to exclude foreigners from the U.S. 200-mile zone while preserving the traditional three-mile zone in South America. This is in contrast to the position taken by coastal fishermen of the Northeast, who are unanimous in their dedication to an Exclusive Economic Zone.

To further complicate matters, the salmon fishermen propose that their ocean fishery be unfished, so that the salmon may be harvested upon their return to protected northwest waters shortly before their breeding time.

Alaska has yet another perception. Alaskan fishermen share with New England the desire for an Exclusive Economic Zone for the king crab and demersal species. One of their richest resources, the pollack, has little commercial value on the mainland but is extremely popular in Japan. A regime is thus sought to assure the availability of the species to the Japanese market and profit to the U.S. entrepreneur.

The varied interests of the United States are embodied in the Fisheries Conservation and Management Act (FCMA). This act was intended to be a model for the UN, but was a model the UN did not follow. It extends U.S. jurisdiction for the management of fisheries to 200 miles. Two kinds of commissions are established — regional and scientific. Acting on the advice of the scientific commissions, the regional commissions establish for each species a "maximum sustainable yield" and an "optimal sustainable yield." They also assess the U.S. fishing industry's capability for each species. The excess is to be allocated to foreign fleets on the basis of their requests, taking account of their prior use of the fisheries.

In principle, the plans and the allocations are made by the secretary of commerce. In practice, the regional commissions (composed of politicians, fishermen, fish processors, and port officials) provide the basic plan. The basic plan satisfies the control desires of the coastal fishermen and the negotiation requirements of the shrimpmen. To placate the tuna fishermen the act specifically defines pelagic fish as only tuna — and then exempts them from the act. To satisfy the salmon fishermen, jurisdiction over salmon that originate in U.S. waters is extended to cover them beyond 200 miles, wherever they may be. The act is thus all things to all fishing interests.

The difficulties in execution are already apparent. The most fundamental problem is the estimate of maximum sustainable yield. Marine biologists are simply not capable of making such an estimate, except for a few species such as corals (which grow like trees) or live bearers (such as sharks). The simple and basic model assumes that the annual recruitment is proportional to the size of the stock; it is fallacious. Only a small fraction of the fish that spawn will survive in the open ocean. The fraction is highly dependent upon oceanographic and climatic conditions and can vary from year to year. Thus the annual recruitment and the size of the stock may not be proportional at all. The late John Isaacs of Scripps Institution has shown that the season-to-season appearances of stocks of sardine and anchovy in the vicinity of Monterey Bay are related to long-term temperature cycles, and the economically disastrous drop in population of the anchovetta off the coast of Chile is now thought to be related to the abnormal behavior of El Nino, the equatorial wind.[14]

Despite these uncertainties, the law requires that the scientific commissions determine the "maximum sustainable" yield. This is at best a bad guess by frustrated scientists. The commissions must then employ environmental, social, and economic criteria to arrive at an "optimal yield," which may be less than, equal to, or in excess of the "maximum sustainable yield." The temptation to yield to political considerations in making an uncertain determination is often irresistible.

A case in point arises from the desire of the Hawaii regional commission to eliminate or drastically reduce Japanese tuna fishing within the 200-mile zone. This is both a legal and policy proscription of the Act. However, a fact of fishing life is that the catch of tuna will include an incidental catch of billfish. The scientific commission has concluded that the catch of billfish in the economic zone is so small that no quota is justified. Nevertheless, the regional commission is proposing a "billfish plan" whose net effect is to further restrict tuna fishing in the 200-mile zone.

In administering the FMCA, cost constraints must be added to the scientific difficulties. For several small species the cost of preparing the management plan has exceeded the value of the catch. The total cost of administering the act is more than the fees received from fishing licenses. Enforcement and the cost of enforcement are major problems yet to be faced. The Coast Guard and the Department of Commerce are officially confident that the act is working effectively. Currently, there are official observers on about 20 percent of the foreign ships in the 200-mile zone. It is too early to assess the government's ability to keep a cadre of inspectors continuously at sea as the sole (and adverse) "alien" observers on ships with hard-working officers and crew. Interviews with a few of the young people who have been on such a mission as inspectors and observers reveal that they had an interesting experience they would not want to repeat. Arrests of crews of ships fishing illegally in the zone have been made and at least one major case of underreporting has been uncovered. In all cases stiff fines were successfully levied, but the arrest, detention, and diplomatic costs were high.

A number of other disturbing factors are present. There are many more license requests than are realistic for the existing quotas; foreign nations have not utilized a significant portion of the quotas; and catches reported "outside" zones of national jurisdiction have dramatically increased.

The Pelagic Game

Only the United States has devised and promulgated such a complex and sophisticated regime as that of the FMCA. Many other nations (altogether 89 of the 120 coastal nations) have established economic zones of 200 miles in which fish are regulated. In all of these zones, the management includes pelagic fish as they pass through the zones. Island nations without the capital or technical infrastructure to exploit their own resources are eager to sell fishing rights in the zone. Negotiations have already taken place between the Federated States of Micronesia and the Japanese, and they are under way between U.S. interests and various island entities in the South Pacific. In view of the migratory nature of tuna as the major resource, their journey through international waters, and the large number of island nations seeking hard currency, the fishing nations and their major commercial fishers are driving hard bargains (as seen from the island perspective). This has been a factor in uniting the nations of the South Pacific Forum in an attempt to create a regional organization that would have complete management control of the South Pacific tuna stocks. These stocks are as yet underutilized and are therefore of great interest to distant water commercial fishing interests.

If one draws 200-mile circles around the islands of the South Pacific Forum (see Figure 6), most but not all of the South Pacific waters of interest will be seen to fall within the combined 200-mile jurisdictions. The dilemma of the Forum is bimodal: (1) the island nations can create a regime that is completely regional but must then allow the United States, Japan, Korea, and other "distant water fishing states" in the Pacific Basin to become parties to the agreement; or, (2) they can create a regime with overlapping and disputed 200-mile zones. In the former instance there will be an opportunity for

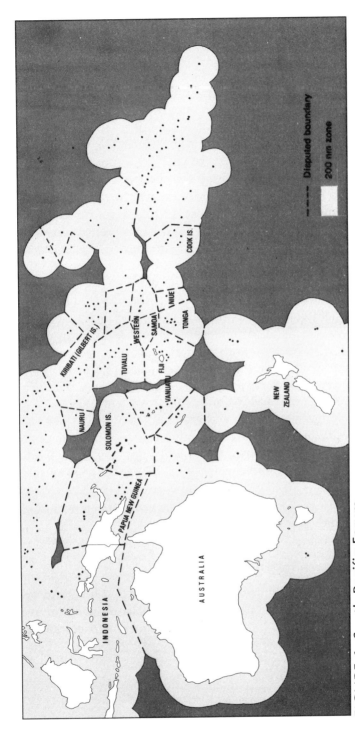

FIGURE 6 South Pacific Forum

cooperation with the fishing nations to secure capital investment in canneries and the assets and technology for enforcement. In the latter instance, there will be a substantial irregularly shaped hole in the center of a doughnut that is international water, and such large quantities of tuna may be "caught in the international zone" that inspection and enforcement will be nonexistent. In either event, the opportunity for fishing nations and economic entities to participate in the harvest of the resource will be substantial.

Fortunately, the game of "access to the resource" is not a zero-sum game. Many techniques exist or have the potential for being developed to increase the quantity of the resource and the ease with which it is harvested. Among these are the development of fish-aggregating (passive) and fish-attractant (active; sound, odor, light) buoys; the development of atypical habitats (such as tropical reefs and cages), genetic breeding to develop new migratory patterns for salmon; techniques for spawning, breeding, and growing juveniles in hatcheries to guarantee adequate annual recruitment for a wide variety of species; development of techniques of artificial upwelling; and utilization of other protein sources such as krill. It has been estimated that total productivity of the ocean could be raised to 2,000 million metric tons per year. These technological and capital-intensive techniques will not be developed unless the developer has access to the resource. But availability of capital and know-how will be a powerful incentive for port states and coastal jurisdictions to negotiate arrangements suitable to the developer.

Exhortations in the Draft Treaty

One might well conclude from this sketch that the ocean as a commons for living resources has disappeared, and that its restoration is at best problematical. A *de facto* commons may, however, evolve from the regime of the Exclusive Economic Zone as a result of technological, economic, political, and social pressures. The language of exhortation in UNCLOS III clearly calls for such a regime:

Article 62
Utilization of the Living Resources

3. In giving access to other States to its exclusive economic zone under this article, the coastal State shall take into account all relevant factors, including, *inter alia*, the significance of the living resources of the area to the economy of the coastal State concerned and its other national interests, the provisions of articles 69 and 70, the requirements of developing States in the subregion or region in harvesting part of the surplus and the need to minimize economic dislocation in States whose nationals have habitually fished in the zone or which have made substantial efforts in research and identification of stocks.[15]

Article 69
Right of Land-locked States

1. Land-locked States shall have the right to participate, on an equitable basis, in the exploitation of an appropriate part of the surplus of the living resources of the exclusive economic zones of coastal States of the same subregion or region, taking into account the relevant economic and geographical circumstances of all States concerned and in conformity with the provisions of this article and of articles 61 and 62.[16]

Article 70
Rights of States with Special Geographical Characteristics

1. States with special geographical characteristics shall have the right to participate, on an equitable basis, in the exploitation of an appropriate part of the surplus of the living resources of the exclusive economic zones of coastal States of the same subregion or region, taking into account the relevant economic and geographical circumstances of all the States concerned and in conformity with the provisions of this article and of articles 61 and 62.[17]

Although these rights are easily defeated by coastal states that invoke the harvesting-capability provision of the treaty, most developing countries do not in fact have such capabilities. Thus, most coastal states will have to enter joint-venture agreements with one or more of the few technologically capable fishing nations. These nations need access to the resource in order to meet their own dietary requirements and preferences. If economic stress is equated to equitable access and if coastal states are willing to provide full access to economically capable nations, then the ideal of the regulated commons will have been approached. However, it is doubtful that the priorities, the yields, or the equities will be established with international fairness as the prime criterion.

Where You Stand Depends on Where You Sit

Two contrasting perceptions—that of Korea, a distant water fishing nation, and that of the South Pacific Forum, a regional administration whose jurisdiction encompasses a significant portion of the South Pacific tuna resource—highlight the gap between reality and rationalization.

Dr. Choung Il Chee of Korea contributed to the Pacific Basin workshop in Tokyo a paper entitled "Sharing of Fisheries Resources between the Coastal and Other States: Towards Equity." He puts the case this way:

> The final triumph for the claim of coastal fisheries jurisdiction came when UNCLOS III . . . adopted the Draft Convention on the Law of the Sea in 1980 . . . whereby the coastal state is given a sovereign right to control its resources within 200-mile Exclusive Economic Zones. Thus an evolution in the unilateralism of coastal state rights over natural resources in the Exclusive Economic Zone became *fait accompli*. It was a remarkable evolution, in that it has taken place at the expense of the right of other states whose distant water fishing fleets used to operate in the Exclusive Economic Zone of the coastal state. The lack of balance in the fishing rights between the coastal and noncoastal states is evident under the Draft Convention on the Law of the Sea: the distant water fishing nations are now deprived of their fishing grounds due to the adoption of a 200-mile fishing zone by coastal states, where coastal states are to exercise sovereign

rights over natural resources. This is quite contrary to justice and equity for the noncoastal states whose fishing interests should have been adequately safeguarded under law. Now that the Draft Convention on the Law of the Sea is in a final stage and that state practices of a 200-mile fishing zone have become *fait accompli*, it may be difficult to restore a proper balance for the rights of noncoastal states. But a reflection on the needs for equitable balance in the fishing interests of both coastal and noncoastal states may serve a useful purpose for the development of rule of law in the interest of international community.[18]

The Draft Convention on the Law of the Sea that has finally emerged under UNCLOS III after seven years of work has not brought out a balanced version of resource sharing between the coastal and noncoastal states. The Convention as a whole tilts towards favoring the fishing interests of the coastal state at the expense of the rights of noncoastal states by recognizing the sovereign rights of coastal states to natural resources within their EEZ. The regime of EEZ is declared as the specific legal regime under Article 55 of the Draft Convention. The coastal state has the right to determine not only the allowable catch, but also the harvesting capacity of the fisheries resources in the EEZ. Noncoastal states are only allowed their access to the surplus of fisheries resources after the coastal state has determined the allowable catch and its harvesting capacity. Thus the unilateralism of the coastal state's right to natural resources within its EEZ is so complete that the right of noncoastal states to the EEZ of the coastal state is no longer a right of any substance.[19]

An equitable sharing of fisheries resources requires that the countries whose dependence on fisheries for the supply of more than 50 percent of animal protein should be given a special consideration in their demand for an access to the EEZs of other states. Japan, the Republic of Korea, Taiwan, and many countries of South and Southeast Asia belong to countries of such category. The Draft Convention on the Law of the Sea does make a reference to such situation by providing that "the nutritional needs of the population of the respective States" should be taken into account in giving access to certain countries under Articles 69 and 70 of the Convention, but such provisions are confined to the land-locked states and states with special geographical characteristics, and they did not go far enough to cover other distant water fishing nations.[20]

Current development on the law of the sea demonstrates that the rights of the coastal state have progressively expanded to an almost exclusive right to control fisheries within its EEZ. On the other hand, the access right of other states has been correspondingly diminished and it has now become restricted to the "surplus" resources. Movement toward this development could be traced to the combination of multiple factors, such as the notion of "adjacency," special dependence on fisheries, and an effective control of fisheries resources. But with the exception of the "adjacency" concept, these criteria are equally applicable to the noncoastal states interested in access to the EEZs of the coastal states. Thus any argument of equity in justification of coastal state sovereign rights to control fisheries resources could also be applied to the noncoastal states. It should be pointed out in this connection that the developing distant water fishing nations are just as dependent on fisheries for their economic livelihood and the supply of food as the coastal states. Between the developed distant water fishing nations and the developing ones, it became fairly clear that developing nations should receive favorable considerations, which may constitute preferential treatment in resource sharing based on equitable principle.

Unfortunately, current state practices demonstrate that they are much more strict in their policy of restricting the access right of the noncoastal states than what has been provided under the Draft Convention on the Law of the Sea. It is quite probable that such state practices would be crystallized into the rule of customary international law even before the Law of the Sea Convention comes into effect. In light of this development, it may serve a useful purpose to place fisheries interests and the legal rights of noncoastal states in a true perspective.

If the issue of equitable sharing of fisheries resources is to revolve around an impartial determination instead of unilateral determination on the distribution of fisheries resources, such determination should have been entrusted in the law to an impartial third party machinery. It is for this reason that the Draft Convention on the Law of the Sea should have created a Commission on Fisheries, whose function would have been similar to that of the Commission on the Limit of the Continental Shelf, under the Draft Convention of the Law of the Sea. Such Commission would determine, on appeal, the issues of allowable catch, harvesting capacity, and the amount of surplus resource in the EEZ.[21]

Peter Wilson, representing Papua New Guinea and speaking of the common interest of the island nations and territories of the South Pacific Forum, presented a very different perspective to the Tokyo workshop. It is his view that the concept of "Pacific Community" introduced by Prime Minister Ohira legitimized the more limited regional community concept embodied in the concept of the South Pacific Forum. He notes that in 1969 "the independent Pacific island states decided to form their own organization as they felt they were being dominated by the metropolitan powers and needed to form their own group which could better serve their joint objectives. Thus the South Pacific Forum came into existence."[22]

If one presumes that the concept of "Pacific Community" is a long-range goal that will evolve from the coalescence of regional communities then it can be said, as Peter Wilson has said, that Ohira's initiative has placed the idea of institutionalizing regional cooperation on the international agenda and that the organization of the South Pacific Forum was a significant and anticipated event.

It is in this vein that Wilson cites the concept of a regional fisheries organization, first introduced by the Prime Minister of Fiji, Ratu Sir Kamisese Mara, at the Seventh South Pacific Forum at Nauru in July 1976. For a period of three years the Forum nations debated the composition of a proposed fishing agency, deciding whether it was to be limited to Forum nations and to their 200-mile Exclusive Economic Zones, or whether it was to include the "hole in the doughnut" and thus allow participation by distant water fishing nations. Wilson's Tokyo paper continues the story: Having opted for the more restrictive membership, the South Pacific Forum limited its membership to

the following independent states: Australia, Cook Island, Fiji, Kiribati (Gilbert Islands), Nauru, New Zealand, Niue, Papua New Guinea, Solomon Islands, Tonga, Tuvalu, Vanuatu and Western Samoa.

Participating as observers are the Federated States of Micronesia, Marshall Islands, and Palau, the former Trust Territory of the Pacific Islands. This gives a total of sixteen countries. It might also be appropriate to name those islands who do not belong. They are the United States possessions of Hawaii, Saipan, Guam, American Samoa, and part of the Line Islands, the French Polynesian Islands, New Caledonia, and Wallis, and Futuna. Easter Island, a possession of Chile in the Eastern Pacific and a few others account for most of the balance.

The ocean mass encompassed within the South Pacific Forum region would total some ten million square miles or most of the Western and Central Pacific below 10°N latitude. Total catches of tuna from this region increased from 156,200 metric tons in 1970 to 554,000 metric tons in 1979. . . .

As the South Pacific Forum Fisheries Agency only recently became operational it has not yet been possible to achieve the goals of unification and harmonization envisaged by the Leaders of the region.

As a consequence, each of the Member States in whose waters the Distant Water Fishing Nations wish to operate have to negotiate with experienced fisheries personnel who have access to all catch data interpreted in any number of ways which favour their views.

Forum Members trying to get a fair payment for the fish taken from their fisheries zones thus feel frustrated and cheated, as to my knowledge none of them have felt they were actually receiving fair payment for the fish taken within their zones. This feeling is not unjustified.

As stated, some 400–500 million dollars of tuna is being taken from the Forum region each year. If a 'fair' price of 5 percent were paid to the countries in whose waters the fish was taken some 20–25 million in fishing fees would be paid into the region. Such is not the case.

Palau receives $300,000, the Federated States of Micronesia get 2.5 million, the Marshalls receive a million and

Kiribati just got another million. Papua New Guinea received in per-boat fees 1.3 million. So only 6.3 million has actually been received by those countries in whose waters most of the fish is harvested. This comes to only 1.2 percent of the value of the fish harvested.

Papua New Guinea for example received under a per-vessel license system 2.7 percent of the value of the fish harvested in its zone by Japanese vessels. This is not satisfactory to Papua New Guinea government officials and the Japanese have just been so advised.

Papua New Guinea's views on what constitutes fair payment are based on what the fishing companies working in the country say they can pay. Two companies, one Japanese and one American have exported up to 50,000 metric tons of frozen tuna a year and paid 7.5 percent of the f.o.b. value for that tuna to the government.

The Solomon Islands have exported some 15,000 metric tons of skipjack and paid 10 percent export duty to the Solomon Island Government.

The one complaint all locally based companies seem to have in common is that the governments in whose waters they are fishing and developing the resources should not allow access to those waters by foreign based fishermen at rates which are below what the local boats pay.

This seems 'fair' to Papua New Guinea.[23]

Probably it is fair to say that two perspectives highlight the equities and inequities associated with the Exclusive Economic Zones:

1. The distant water fishing fleet faces economic bankruptcy because of the ever-increasing fuel costs, the amortization of fines and penalties "unjustly" imposed, the costs of regulatory license fees, accountancy and bureaucracy, and the denial of access to the resource.

2. The coastal zone state pays the capital and operating costs to develop and maintain the fishery, develops an economic dependency on the profits from the resource and the resource products, pays the costs of regulation and enforcement, and has to face the political problems of competition with its own people. Moreover, the coastal zone state must guard against economic blackmail resulting from monopolies

or near-monopolies of technology and harvesting capability, and must cope with the unfair competition from fishermen who harvest the resource legally in the ocean commons or illegally in the economic zone of the coastal state. Under such a regime both parties are victims of a classic negative-sum game: "my enlightened greed, your unenlightened greed."

5
Transportation Futures
of the Oceans

The discussions on energy, mineral, and living resources included the tacit assumption that the ocean has remained an unregulated commons for transportation. Indeed it has been an assumption if not a determination on the part of the industry that transportation is set apart from other uses of the sea, and that its independence is sacrosanct except for self-imposed regulation.

This notion appears to be embodied in the text of UNCLOS III. Article 17 says: "Subject to this Convention, ships of all States, whether coastal or land-locked, enjoy the right of innocent passage through the territorial sea."[24] Article 21:2 adds: "Such laws and regulations [of the Coastal State] shall not apply to the design, construction, manning or equipment of foreign ships unless they are giving effect to generally accepted international rules or standards."[25]

The realities of vessel-source pollution and the extensive damage that can be done to the environment and the coastal zone as a result of accidents at sea, the realities of high-speed navigation and high traffic density in accepted sea lanes and in straits and port entries, and the capabilities of modern technology have eroded—and ought to erode—many of the traditional freedoms of transportation. Although the independence of the user community is protected with respect to pollution-protection measures by limiting enforcement to the "flag state" (i.e., the state that grants nationality and registration to a ship) and the "port state," (i.e., the state or port to which a ship is bound), Article 220 provides specific "coastal state" opportunities for enforcement as in paragraph 2 of the Article:

> 2. Where there are clear grounds for believing that a vessel navigating in the territorial sea of a State has, during its passage therein, violated laws and regulations of that State adopted in accordance with this Convention or applicable international rules and standards for the prevention, reduction and control of pollution from vessels, that State, without prejudice to the application of the relevant provisions of Part II section 3 may undertake physical inspection of the vessel relating to the violation and may, where the evidence so warrants, institute proceedings, including detention of the vessel, in accordance with its laws, subject to the provisions of section 7.[26]

And in paragraph 6 of the same Article the jurisdiction of the coastal state is further broadened to include the EEZ.

> 6. Where there is clear objective evidence that a vessel navigating in the exclusive economic zone or the territorial sea of a State has, in the exclusive economic zone, committed a violation, referred to in paragraph 3, resulting in a discharge causing major damage or threat of major damage to the coastline or related interest of the coastal State, or to any resources of its territorial sea or exclusive economic zone, that State may, subject to the provisions of section 7, provided that the evidence so warrants, institute proceedings, including detention of the vessel, in accordance with its laws.[27]

Dr. Edgar Gold expanded upon this theme of commons pollution and traffic in his conference presentation entitled "Marine Transportation in the Pacific." Specifically he referred to commons accidents, regulatory measures, and traffic control systems, outlining both his views and developments thus:

> One of the most important factors affecting shipping in the last one and a half decades has been the discernible trend to protect the marine environment. Although at least 90 percent

of all marine pollution originates from land-based sources, the major concentration, at least until very recently, has been against the remaining 10 percent. . . . However, the overall effect of this trend on shipping is, and will be, felt as keenly in the Pacific as elsewhere. Apart from the SHOWA MARU grounding, the region has so far been preserved from major tanker disasters of the AMOCO CADIZ dimension and notoriety. That has been due to luck more than anything else. The "Asian rim" oil transportation to Japan from the Middle East has to transit several danger spots, ranging from the shallows of the Straits of Malacca, the currents of the Sunda and Lombok channels to the traffic density and high accident rate of the Japanese waters. In addition, some of the oil and LNG loading facilities in Indonesia, Borneo, and Sarawak are in shallow, tricky, and dangerous navigable waters. Finally, seasonal, meteorological phenomena, such as monsoon strength and the prevalence of tropical revolving storms, such as typhoons, further contribute to the fact that a statistical time bomb is ticking away on a very major Pacific tanker disaster. The preventative response from Pacific littoral states ranges from Canada (and to a lesser extent, the U.S.A.), with some of the strictest marine pollution regulations in the world, to states in the South Pacific which have none at all. . . .

The Inter-Governmental Maritime Consultative Organization (IMCO), which commenced life as a small technical/advisory United Nations body, but has now become a 121 member organization devoted to the principle of "clean seas and safe ships," can now react with regulatory patterns, probably more restrictive than they might have been or needed to be. . . .

First, the ships themselves will have to be safer and, thus, also more expensive. New anti-pollution technology, clean ballast systems and double bottoms will soon be mandatory. This will eventually drive the fly-by-night companies, often operating out of Hong Kong and Singapore and utilizing very elderly tonnage, from the seas . . . Secondly, on the human front, IMCO's tightening of training standards for seamen and officers will also bring about changes. The Pacific area, particularly Indonesia, Philippines, Hong Kong, and Taiwan, has, for some time, been a major supplier of ship personnel. Some have been highly skilled seamen, but others have been used as cheap labour. The new standards will even out these differences and may force some states into a more organized marine training system, perhaps on a regional, cooperative basis. This human element should not be dismissed lightly. Statistics show us that some 90 percent of all marine accidents occur because of human error.

Thirdly, the most comprehensive change to traditional marine transportation in the Pacific area will be the establishment of new marine traffic control systems, particularly in areas of high traffic density such as the Sea of Japan and other semi-enclosed seas on the west Pacific rim. These will range from "full control systems" (akin to air traffic control) in port approaches and narrow straits, to traffic separation zones, where warranted by traffic. It can be conceded that this innovation is, of course, an almost complete abrogation of the hallowed freedom-of-the-seas principle, which ostensibly gave a master power "between God and the sea" to take his ship where and how he wished. However, the ever-increasing curve of the burgeoning world fleet, dissected by ever-increasing shipping accidents, has convinced IMCO that, some half century after compulsory air traffic control, an embryonic similar system for maritime transport was indicated.

As expected, resistance by the shipping states has been strong, and IMCO's lowest common denominator approach has been unsatisfactory for a number of coastal states, such as Canada, the U.S.A., and the Malacca Straits countries. This has resulted in a certain amount of unilateralism which has, nevertheless, set the pattern for things to come. On the Canadian-U.S. west coast, the jointly administered Puget Sound traffic system has operated successfully for some years, and the Malacca Strait system, due to go into full operation later this year, is expected to provide the type of vessel safety control that has reduced accidents in the English Channel by 45 percent. The Malacca Strait states are assisted by the Malacca Strait Council, which basically attempts to achieve a compromise between the hard line anti-pollution policies of littoral states and the Japanese interests in the Malacca lifeline. Without doubt, marine traffic control will quickly establish itself as its safety statistics will speak for themselves. It can be foreseen that further marine traffic control systems will be established in the Hawaiian archipelago, on the Australian coast, in all the enclosed seas off the Asian mainland, in the main Indonesian straits, as well as the Indonesian and Philippine archipelagic zones, and in the approaches to the Panama Canal. It is unlikely that the systems will be extended beyond 200-mile exclusive economic zones in the foreseeable future. On the other hand, the costs of the new system can be considerable, and coastal states will inevitably not only require these systems to be established where warranted but will also ask the users to pay for them.[28]

This "creeping jurisdiction"of coastal states designated in UNCLOS III — on the one hand preventive medicine against commons pollution and accidents, and on the other, a conscious limitation of transportation freedoms — not only converges with the self-regulatory mechanism of IMCO but also that of the United Nations Conference on Trade and Development (UNCTAD). Gold, in his conference presentation, expounded in this vein with a knowledgeable "shipping weather prognosis,"[29] stating his views as follows:

The Pacific marine transportation pattern is, of course, closely allied to existing international trading relationships. In this context, we must speak of blocks of nations — such as the U.S.A. and Japan; Australia/New Zealand and Canada; China and the Southeast and East Asian states; the South Pacific islands and Latin American Pacific states, in order of maritime and trading importance. When the actual, established shipping routes are examined, it is found that over 50 percent of Pacific shipping moves on the Asian rim — particularly from the Middle East to Japan; about 30 percent moves in true trans-Pacific fashion from the west coast of North America to Central America, and after transiting the Panama Canal, to Asia, Australia, and Oceania. The remainder consists of cross-trading, local shipping, and tramp shipping. It is unlikely that this pattern is going to change greatly in the foreseeable future. . . .

First and foremost, Japan's insatiable energy and resource hunger will increase further. . . . This need is fed by Japan's general economic prosperity, which has become almost independent of world economic conditions. In other words, the "shipping pipeline" along the Asian coast from the Middle

East to Japan will increase rather than abate. Furthermore, oil and gas from Indonesia, coal and other minerals from Australia and Canada and from the U.S. via Panama to Japan, will continue to keep shipowners very happy. In the other direction, Japan's mighty industrial output will provide manufactured goods cargoes to all parts of the world. There is likely to be intensification of bulk resource exports from Australia to Japan. In addition, U.S. and Canadian coal exports to Japan will, due to Japanese investment, also increase further. Also, the further development of Indonesian oil and the likely opening up of energy resources in Papua/New Guinea will give additional incentives to the shipping of these cargoes — again, mostly to Japan. The present slump in the LNG (liquid natural gas) trade between Indonesia and Japan is of a momentary nature. It will soon swing back to full production once oil prices have achieved some discernible stabilization. On the Eastern rim, maritime transport developments will be much slower as there is traditionally little trade down the American coast — north and south. However, the consolidation of Pemex in Mexico as a world oil-trading concern, and the development of the Ecuadorian oil fields, might spur some discernible developments in shipping in the region.

Regular liner trades, using the latest-generation, super container vessels, are probably saturated for the foreseeable future. It is quite likely that the present overtonnaging might even result in the reduction of services. The acceptance of the UNCTAD Liner Trade Code of Conduct 40:40:20 cargo-sharing principle will certainly hurt some traditional shipping lines based in the United States, United Kingdom, Japan, and Norway, but will benefit the expanding Soviet cargo liner fleets as well as those of Korea, People's Republic of China, Indonesia, Philippines, and possibly, Australia. It must also be borne in mind that the world's most formidable corporate concentration of shipping is now resident in the Singapore/ Hong Kong axis, and it remains to be seen what UNCTAD's attempt to phase out "flags of convenience" or "open registries" — at present almost violently resisted by UNCTAD's "B-group" (OECD [Nuclear Energy Agency, U.S.A.] group), will mean. Unfortunately, the UNCTAD versus status-quo shipping industry confrontation will have no winners, as commercial intransigence by one group has already led to political inflexibility in the other. There is no doubt that if UNCLOS III is the law-reform movement of the "public" uses of the ocean, then, in a more subdued way, UNCTAD is attempting to realign the *control* of world shipping in a more equitable way. For the 200-odd million tons of shipping in the Pacific trade, the repercussions could be problematic if the continuing lack of understanding by the UNCTAD B-group prevails. It has to be remembered that very important resource countries, such as the People's Republic of China, Indonesia and Mexico, are highly visible members of the Group of 77 at UNCTAD.[30]

In summary of the commons transportation and pollution issues we conclude that it may be characteristic of human society that preventive action will be taken only after disaster occurs and not before. Yet the technology now exists for safe ships, for full routing and traffic control throughout ocean space, for accurate navigation on the high seas, and for continuous and high-volume communications through oceanic space. Advantages do accrue, and will increasingly accrue, to operators who will pay the cost of a strictly regulated regime in return for a monopoly within a given transportation network. This has been true for a number of years in the United States where the Jones Act limits shipping to U.S. flag ships built in the United States and manned by U.S. crews.

6
Ocean Technology Futures

The ability to use the ocean as a commons, or to deny its use, is very largely a function of the state of technology. This is amply demonstrated in our consideration of energy, minerals, living resources, and transportation. Technology also permeates every other phase of ocean use—for military purposes, for recreational purposes, as a sink for waste disposal, as a medium for aesthetic enjoyment, for psychological attachment, or simply as open space. A general understanding of new developments in ocean technology may thus provide additional insight about the future management of the Pacific Marine Commons.

Two types of technological developments are foreseeable: technology for everyone's use (that is, available to indigenous economies), and technologies that are capital-intensive and require capital and technology transfer in order to be used by developing nations.

Small-Scale, Indigenous Technologies

At the indigenous level the most significant technological advances are the following:

- *Development of low-cost, long-lived materials and fabrication techniques for construction of ships and structures.* Most prominent is fiberglass for use as a primary structural material for boat hulls, tanks, hatcheries, containers, and perhaps more significantly, as a coating for repair, preservation, and protection from corrosion, biological fouling, toxic materials, etc.

- *Development of plastic materials, especially the poly-mers (polyurethane, polyethylene, and polypropylene).* Plastic pipes, valves, pumps, etc., are an absolute re-quirement for biological systems to avoid toxicity or the introduction of metal contaminants into the food chain. Polymers, acrylics, and other plastics, such as Teflon and nylon, have major application for noncor-rosive coatings, transparent hulls and ports, ropes and connectors, and bushings. A major and most signifi-cant development is in foams that provide buoyancy and nonsinkable properties for hulls and equipment. The lightweight, buoyant surfboard is, for example, a highly developed structural sandwich of fiberglass, laminates, and buoyancy foams in an optimized hydrodynamic configuration. With proper training, in-water personnel can use it as a sophisticated sea sled.

- *Development and availability of satellite navigation and communication systems.* Now, and in the near future, increasingly sophisticated weather and climate maps and advisories should be available on a world, re-gional, and local basis by means of satellite communi-cations. Technical advisory services and seminars are in embryonic form (as in the Hawaii-based educational satellite system called PeaceSat) but are rapidly devel-oping on a global basis. Satellite navigation is also widely available, but the currently available commercial receivers are oversophisticated and, as a consequence, needlessly expensive. Another part of the communica-tion revolution is the development of short-range, line-of-sight, accurate, and high-bit-rate navigation and communication systems. Precision location of nets, traps, buoys, etc., is now economically feasible. When coupled with transponder systems, these navigation and communication systems can provide security as well as efficiency in the harvesting of common prop-erty resources.

- *Development and availability of low-cost high-bit-rate computer systems.* This revolution applies to almost every aspect of personal, local, regional, national, and international life and cannot be ignored in projecting the future of any human system. When combined with a telecommunications network (even as unsophisticated as the local telephone system), the computer terminal, coupled with central and peripheral computers and sensors, provides means to manage and monitor the entire oceanic system. Catastrophe, predation, and disease are costly to fishery and oceanographic operation. A communication-computer network can provide information and warnings that greatly reduce these costs. This is true also for television-monitoring systems. Costs are decreasing for these technologies and thus their use will soon be ubiquitous.

- *Sensors and life-support equipment.* A host of sensors and life-support equipment for humans as well as for use with marine animals and other organisms are commercially available. The underwater swimmer has an ever-growing array of scuba equipment and life-support systems — diver vehicles, communication equipment, wet suits, decompression facilities, swimmer support vehicles, etc. Sophisticated diving capabilities to a depth of 50 to 60 meters are thus available. The black coral and abalone fisheries have employed divers, but the use of divers in other ocean applications has been needlessly limited. To dive deeper than 60 meters requires mixed gas and probably is too sophisticated to be introduced at the indigenous, small scale level. But the techniques for monitoring dissolved oxygen, pH, water chemistry, free oxygen, other gases, pollutants, etc., are well developed and commercially available.

- *Developments in energy sources and power plants.* Relatively few of the developments in power and energy will be available at the indigenous level. For tropical countries (i.e., most developing nations) it should be possible to manufacture alcohol without a net deficit in oil imports. The commercial availability of engines designed and modified to use gasohol or alcohol as a result of the U.S. energy program or the Brazil alcohol program could provide a net energy benefit. (This will be particularly true if power systems are available for low-proof alcohols.)

- *Development of OTEC with resulting changes in the indigenous energy picture.* As previously discussed in detail, ammonia is a suitable fuel for automotive equipment (with only slight modifications), and the ammonia fuel cell would be a simple, easily maintained source of central power for the smallest of rural power systems. Even a small (100 Megawatt) OTEC system would provide energy self-sufficiency for most Pacific oceanic archipelagos (Fiji, Tonga, Cook Islands, Kiribati, etc.).

New Understanding of Ocean Processes

The technological developments just outlined go hand in hand with a new understanding of ocean processes, which of course contributes to the development of the new technologies.

1. *Better environments for living resources.* There is new understanding of the environmental conditions required for spawning, survival of the spawn, hatching, survival of larvae, survival of juveniles, growth of young adults, maturation, etc. Organisms of a number of species have been carried through their life cycles in the laboratory (*Macrobrachium rosenbergii*, mullet, milkfish, salmon, mahi mahi, oysters, clams), and others have been carried through substages that permit farming (*Penneus japonicus*, *Penneus marginatus*, sturgeon, yellowtail, unagi). The possibilities are increasing rapidly, species by species. Technologies that are needed include hatcheries, holding pens, and—where the cost of feeding is prohibitive—open-sea cages or pond and bay environments in which predators and disease can be controlled.

2. *Fish behavior.* There is also new understanding of pelagic and migratory fish behavior. We are increasing our

understanding of migratory patterns, the role of temperature and of temperature gradients, the role of flotsam in congregating and aggregating behavior, and the role of symbiotic animals — bait fish, dolphins, sea birds — in the schooling and migratory process.

Better knowledge spawns better technology, such as fish-aggregating buoys. The density of fish that collect around these buoys is great enough to have commercial significance. A number of innovative designs and deployments are certain to follow; the tuna yield in the Philippines has already substantially increased as a result of evolutionary development of raft and line aggregation devices. Future related developments include the use of fish attractants, bait fish, and modified configurations to enhance both attraction potential and multispecies potential of the buoys. Further evolution of purse-seining techniques can also be expected. The current technology of winches, blocks, tackle, nets, launchers, seines, etc., already employs modern materials and structures. Techniques have been developed for permitting and encouraging captured porpoises to escape before the seine is closed.

Such improvements in seining and in long liningpole and bait fishing are, however, evolutionary changes from old techniques. The fullest understanding of the herding and aggregating process will permit substitution of mechanical gate and enclosure devices that are more closely matched to existing on-board storage and processing techniques.

3. *Management of nutrients.* There is new understanding of the assimilation process for wastes and of the aggregation and dilution of nutrients in ocean environments. As a result of environmental concerns, a better understanding of the effects of waste discharge in ocean waters is emerging. From recent studies conducted by the Southern California Water Resources Research Project (SCWRRP), Woods Hole Oceanographic Institute, and the University of Hawaii, marine biologists now recognize that with appropriate attention to waste system inputs and with the proper outfall configurations, waste effluents can greatly enhance food-fish populations.

The problem of viral contamination, which currently limits the use of sewage for feeding shellfish and other filter feeders, may soon be solved by sterilization techniques. In that event, sewage and waste systems can be developed in conjunction with aquaculture, fish-attractants, and fish-farming techniques.

A further supplement to nutrition can be obtained in many tropical and subtropical areas through pumping of deep ocean water to the surface. Novel, low cost devices such as the Isaacs wave pump are available for pumping this water to the surface. A number of schemes have been developed for the use of this water in shellfish culture and in cultivation of opihi, Irish moss, algae, and salt-tolerant plants by using the "trickle" condensate on pipes carrying the deep ocean water.

4. *Safety and predictability.* Other processes whose enhanced understanding will aid fisheries and oceanography include air/sea interaction as it relates to the forecasting of weather and climate, geophysical and oceanographic conditions that pinpoint the location of an animal or mineral resource, and new methods of food processing and preservation. Modern technology for use in coastal waters and the coastal zone is advancing at the indigenous level and will greatly benefit resource development in remote or hazardous sea environments. As the present handicaps of remoteness and peril are reduced, fishery and oceanic alternatives to land-based food production and resource development become more attractive to a developing society.

Large-Scale, Capital-Intensive Technologies

At the other end of the spectrum — that of large-scale capital investment — marine technology now will permit the development of major support systems for society that appear to be economically competitive and environmentally sound. Because they will be sea-based, they can be introduced into a developing society without the necessity for also developing an expensive land-based infrastructure or capital base, and they will probably cost less and consume less energy than their land-based counterparts.

These oceanic systems include: (1) oceanic energy production systems; (2) ocean energy processing and transportation
systems; (3) sea-based industrial systems; (4) open-sea mariculture and fishing systems; (5) ocean mining systems; (6)
marine transportation systems for bulk, containerized, liquid, dry, and gaseous cargoes; (7) urban mass transit systems;
(8) riverine and sea-based public works and public utility
systems; (9) sea-based waste disposal systems; (10) floating
hotels, condominiums, office complexes, and shopping cen-
ters; and (11) sea-based park and recreation systems.

The most significant technical development—stable ocean
platforms—has decoupled sea systems from the surface of
the sea and, as a consequence, has eliminated or alleviated the
debilitating motions associated with sea-based operations.
The development is significant because it accommodates
equipment, techniques, and life styles previously suited only
to a low-motion, land-based environment. Not only the dis-
comforts but also the perils of the sea are nearly eliminated
by this development.

Five mechanisms have been employed to achieve this
result:

1. The use of very large conventional carriers and conventional displacement forms. For displacement of not less than
40,000 tons—ideally 100,000 tons or more—conventional
hull forms will provide a platform sufficiently stable for
nearly every social or industrial process (except billiards) in
all but extreme sea conditions.

2. The use of semisubmerged (small waterplane area) platforms and semisubmerged ships. For displacements of 1,000
to 10,000 tons they will provide a sufficiently stable platform
for nearly every social or industrial process in all but extreme
sea conditions.

3. The use of semisubmerged platforms with displacements of 10,000 tons or more. The stability of these platforms is satisfactory for nearly every social or industrial
process (including billiards) in all weather conditions.

4. The use of incidence-control hydrofoils or fin-stabilized
semisubmersibles controlled by a control system with sea-
surface sensors. These structures can support a mobile plat-

form of satisfactory stability for high-speed (50 knots) transfer of goods and people with adequate comfort.

5. The use of submarines at a depth of 500 feet or more.
These submersibles will support platforms of adequate stability for nearly every social or industrial process in all sea
conditions.

Accompanying the development of the stable platform has
been the development of prestressed concrete for very large
structures. This development has appeared in large semisub-
mersible structures designed for oil storage and processing in
the North Sea. The construction of these structures and their
successful deployment in one of the most hazardous of ocean
environments demonstrates that large ocean structures
(1,000,000 tons) can be manufactured at one site for use in a
remote location.

The possible uses for such stable platforms and barges are
legion. Japanese industry has already built a power plant and
a paper mill on barges in Japan for use on a river in Brazil.
(Symbolically, the deployment was antipodal.) In its river
operation in Brazil the project has demonstrated that no major modifications have been required from the previous land-
based mill operation to the new river-based operation. The
wood is floated to the barge, and the processed paper is carried away by a transport barge to the distribution port. This
paper mill could just as easily have been a fish-processing
facility and cannery.

As already mentioned, the Westinghouse Electric Corporation has been attempting to develop barge-mounted, sea-
based nuclear power plants. Offshore Power Systems, a joint
venture of Westinghouse Electric Corporation and Westinghouse International Power Systems Company, Inc., was
established in Jacksonville, Florida, to manufacture and
secure licensing of eight floating nuclear power plants. Con-
tracts were signed with New Jersey's Public Service Electric
and Gas Company in September 1971 for construction of the
first two plants and in November 1973 for two more plants. A
combination of environmental, political, and financial pressures, along with estimates of reduced growth in demand for
electricity, led to the cancellation of those initial orders in

December 1978. Although Offshore Power Systems currently has no further orders, it continues to work toward licensing of a standardized manufacturing process for the production of floating nuclear power plants.

Other systems developed for mounting on barges and semi-submersibles include plants for liquefying natural gas and drilling rigs for scientific and commercial use.

Complementing the semisubmerged platform is the semi-submerged platform (SSP) ship. The high-speed, low-drag, stable-surface ship sacrifices above-water payload for its superior performance in sea-keeping energy conservation, i.e., eliminating the energy penalty caused by wave-making For most missions, except bulk cargo transport, the above-water payload capacity of the surface ship is underutilized. This is particularly true for car and passenger ferries. The SSP is thus ideal for deep-river, bay, port, coastal, and inter-island transportation of light freight, cars, and passengers. When supported by high-speed hydrofoils for passenger transport and barges for bulk, liquid and dry freight, the total sea-based transportation network in many coastal environments is superior to its land-based counterpart.

It is the large-scale technologies that have made OTEC both feasible and commercially attractive. In its most advanced form, the open-cycle system OTEC will produce large quantities of fresh water as well as power and a supply of artificially upwelled nutrients. Depending upon the developmental perspective, OTEC can be conceived as a major power system with aquaculture and fresh water as by-products, or as a mariculture system with power and fresh water as by-products, or as a freshwater producer with power and mariculture as by-products. In a larger, longer-range context, these three ingredients added to the stable space available on large-scale platforms provide the fundamental ingredients for a community on the high seas beyond the areas of national jurisdiction.

Floating or slowly mobile communities operating on the high seas will raise new sets of jurisdictional problems. Who is entitled to the increased productivity in the vicinity of the community, when such productivity has been occasioned by the increase in nutrient concentration and improved habitat provided by the community itself? What forms of pollution control or "zones of mixing" associated with each community will be tolerable on a world basis? What are the "rules of the road" for these communities vis-à-vis conventional shipping and other slowly mobile and relatively uncontrollable communities? To what extent is this use of ocean space an entitlement of the Pacific commons, and does this entitlement apply to every class of economic, social, or sovereign entity? The list of questions is long and provides the grist for many future workshops and international fora.

7
The Ocean Commons:
Try Again in the Pacific?

Our understanding of the technological and physical nature of the Pacific Marine Commons leads to consideration of its institutional implications.

The content of the ocean-as-a-commons metaphor has undergone a dramatic transformation over the past decade. In Garrett Hardin's original concept[31] the "tragedy of the commons" develops when no regime emerges to inhibit private party raids on the commons, the public land that everyone has right to. In a vivid example Hardin shows what the inevitable outcome will be when overgrazing occurs (parallel to our ocean-grazing but land-based — the commons is a pasture). Unless there are clear sanctions to force every farmer to limit the size of his own herd, the *only* choice an individual farmer has when the quality of his herd deteriorates is to increase the number of animals. Such action by individual farmers leads to depletion of the commons resource as a whole, which leads in turn to disaster for the people who depend on the commons for their livelihood and sustenance.

When serious attention turned to the management of ocean resources, only a decade or so ago, the fear of depletion of ocean resources quickly became "received wisdom." The question asked was not how marine animals and plants, seabed minerals, and energy resources should be distributed, but whether humankind could avoid depleting them as a whole. But the lesson of the past decade, codified in the conclusions of the Tokyo workshop in June 1981, is that the distribution of resources is, in fact, the primary issue. *The real question is: Who is going to reap what proportion of the yield of the seas at what cost?*

The new "tragedy of the commons" is the tendency to chop the commons into manageable pieces, thereby risking its resources *not* being exploited for the benefit of humankind, but instead being wasted; intensifying preexisting inequities and providing a whole set of new occasions for international conflict.

Coastal states now proceed to regulate fishing catches, claim the oil resources, and jealously guard their seabeds and transportation routes. The result may well have to be another but different attempt to *create* a Pacific marine commons during the 1980s.

In fact, only a very few coastal states now can claim the capacity to police their 200-mile zones, and their efforts are partly symbolic. Even the United States and Japan have difficulty in effectively guarding their waters. Fishing fleets regularly move in and out of 200-mile zones. Only multinational oil companies appear to have control of the information and technology associated with offshore exploration. A very few companies, based in even fewer countries, have the capacity to harvest seabed minerals — and they face so uncertain a legal environment in the ocean commons that they are bound to be hesitant about investing the huge sums involved. Above all the "sea grab" has greatly extended the zones of conflict between coastal states. This is true, for example, among the ASEAN states. Presently many states confront each other's borders directly.

Hence new international rivalries, unregulated operations of multinational companies, and most nations' foreknowledge that they will not be able to exploit "their" resources in the foreseeable future, are likely to lead to a growing conviction that a real ocean commons is after all more beneficial to nearly all concerned.

Since this has not been accomplished for the world as a whole, maybe there is now a strong case for negotiating a viable regime for the Pacific Commons. The Pacific is not only the largest ocean, but also the richest in resources relevant to the twenty-first century. The next step, which goes beyond the "multilogue" at our Tokyo workshop and beyond the scope of this book — will be to invent, consult about, and eventually negotiate a Pacific Commons that blunts the clearly foreseeable conflict points, enhances needed economic growth in the Pacific region, and spreads the benefits of that growth equitably among the Pacific peoples — "South" as well as "North."

In any event, the idea of the oceans as a commons will not go away. Nor will it be relevant only to "holes in doughnuts" — that is, what is left after all the seaward extension of land-based jurisdictions. Nations have an inherent obligation to exercise their jurisdiction in ways that take the interests of their neighbors into account. That obligation will increasingly be translated into law, whether by customary acts or by formal pacts.

Appendix A
Workshop Participants

Participants in the workshop on "The Management of the Pacific Marine Commons" at the International House of Japan, Tokyo, 25-28 June 1981, were as follows.

Professor Roger Benjamin, Hubert H. Humphrey Institute of Public Affairs, 909 Social Science Tower, 267 19th Avenue South, University of Minnesota, Minneapolis, MN 55455

Ms. Eugenia Bennagen, Chief Researcher, Strategy Research Division, Natural Resources Management Center, Manila, Philippines

Dr. Choung Il Chee, Apartment 503, A-dong San-ik Mansion, Yoido, Yongdongpo-ku, Seoul, Korea

Professor Harlan Cleveland, Director, Hubert H. Humphrey Institute of Public Affairs, 909 Social Science Tower, 267 19th Avenue South, University of Minnesota, Minneapolis, MN 55455

Dr. John P. Craven, 4921 Waa Street, Honolulu, HI 96822

Dr. Edgar Gold, Director of Ocean Studies, Dalhousie University, 1321 Edward Street, Halifax, Nova Scotia B3H 4 9

Professor Julian Gresser, Law School, Harvard University, Cambridge, Massachusetts

Mr. Yasushi Hara, Senior Writer, Asahi Shimbun Publishing Company, 3-2 Tsukiji 5-chome, Chuo-ku, Tokyo 104, Japan

Mr. Michael Hirschfeld, 74 Weld Street, Wadestown, Wellington, New Zealand

Mr. Kent M. Keith, Department of Planning & Economic Development, Manganese Nodules, State of Hawaii, 250 South King Street, P.O. Box 2359, Honolulu, HI 96804

Dr. Frances Lai, Department of Political Science, National University of Singapore, Kent Ridge, Singapore 0511, Republic of Singapore

Dr. Hahn Been Lee, Chairman, The Korea Advanced Institute of Science and Technology, P.O. Box 150, Chongyang, Seoul 131, Korea

Dr. Jorge A. Lozoya, El Colegio de Mexico, A.C., Camino Al Ajusco No. 20, Mexico 20, D. F.

Mr. Mochtar Lubis, 17 Jalan Bonang, Jakarta Pusat, Indonesia

Professor Keiichi Oshima, c/o Technova, Inc., 13th Floor, Fukoku-Seimei Building, 2-2-2 Uchisaiwai-cho, Chiyoda-ku, Tokyo 100, Japan

Dr. Choon-ho Park, Culture Learning Institute, The East-West Center, Honolulu, HI 96848

Dr. Herbert Passin, Special Advisor, Aspen Institute for Humanistic Studies, Home: 25 Claremont Avenue, New York, NY 10027

Professor K. S. Sandhu, Director, Institute of Southeast Asian Studies, Heng Mui Keng Terrace, Pasir Panjang, Singapore 0511, Republic of Singapore

Dr. Seizaburo Sato, Department of Political Science, Faculty of General Education, University of Tokyo, 865 Kowaba, Meguroku, Tokyo, Japan

Dr. Phiphat Tangsubkul, 2230-14th Soi Phayakaporm, Chan Road, Yanava, Bangkok, Thailand

Mr. Masataka Watanabe, National Institute for Environmental Studies, Yatabe, Tsukuba, Ibaraki 305, Japan

Mr. Peter Wilson, Box 123, Port Moresby, Papua New Guinea

Appendix B
Workshop Papers

The following papers were read at the workshop on "The Management of the Pacific Marine Commons," held in Tokyo, 25–28 June 1981.

Chee, Choung Il. Sharing of Fisheries Resources Between the Coastal and Other States: Towards Equity.

Craven, John P. The Ocean as a Commons with Emphasis on Energy.

Gold, Edgar. Marine Transportation in the Pacific.

Keith, Kent M. Marine Mining: Six Scenarios for the Eighties.

Lai, Frances. ASEAN's Perspectives on Managing Pacific Basin Marine Resources: The Case of Energy Development.

Wilson, Peter. The Views of the Pacific Island Nations on the Development of the Fisheries Resources of the Western and Central Pacific Ocean.

Appendix C
Chee Plan

At the conference on "The Management of the Pacific Marine Commons" in Tokyo a good deal of attention was given to listing and defining the ocean-linked questions faced by the countries in the Pacific Basin. These questions have been examined earlier in this monograph and collectively suggest, when one reflects on the development of Atlantic-based institutions over the past 100 years, that we are very likely just at the beginning of an explosion of Pacific-centered activity on all the fronts discussed in this volume. For example, policy questions concerning fishing (e.g., protection of stocks, and rights of those who fish versus the rights of countries contiguous to the fishing grounds) are going to be more, not less, serious in the near future. Is it possible to monitor the fishing areas from the perspective of the Pacific Commons as a whole? For instance, could user-based taxes on fishing fleets, shipping industries, etc., be fairly imposed, enforced and collected, and used to maintain and improve the fishing areas? Could modest resources be used to finance a center that would focus on position studies and specific policy recommendations concerning the import of the issues and trends charted in this study?

One of the participants at the conference, Dr. Choung Il Chee, proposed an imaginative outline for a center for ocean development. The distinctiveness of Dr. Chee's plan rests on the assumption that all Pacific Basin countries *do* share an interest in redefining, perhaps functionally, the dimensions of the Pacific Commons; self-interest warrants development of Pacific-wide perspectives on the vexing bilateral and multilateral questions that are before us already. The Chee Plan is reprinted here as a beginning—the kernel of a comprehensive idea that warrants consideration.

CHEE PLAN

Proposed Organization Scheme for the Pacific Marine Commons

I. Names for the Organization
   A. Pacific Center for Ocean Development
   B. Pacific Center for Ocean Development and Cooperation
   C. Pacific Commission for Ocean Development and Cooperation
II. Proposed Site for the Organization
   A. Manila. This city is not only ideally located in the Pacific, but it also houses the Asia Development Bank and ICLARM (International Center for Living Aquatic Resources Management). ICLARM is concerned with the fisheries problems in the South Pacific and Southeast Asia. Its cooperation with the proposed organization should be very beneficial to the organization.
   B. Alternate sites: Guam, Saipan, Hawaii, and Tokyo
III. Structure
   A. Plenary meeting of all member states with associate member states participating in the deliberations of the meeting without a right to vote. This meeting could be called either the Plenary Meeting or the Council. Each member state will send two delegates, hence have two votes; the delegate pair should include one from the government and the other from the industrial sector. Delegates could vote individually or as a unit.
   B. Secretariat
      1. Department of Planning for Technical Assistance and Cooperation. This body would deal with cooperative and technical assistance planning for needy states.
      2. Department of Living Resources
         a. North Pacific
         b. South Pacific
      3. Department of Nonliving Resources
         a. North Pacific
         b. South Pacific
      4. Department of Energy and Pollution
IV. Membership
   A. Full membership: United States, Japan, Canada, Australia,

New Zealand, Republic of Korea, Philippines, Indonesia, Malaysia, Thailand, Singapore

B. Associate members: 16 microstates in the Pacific
C. Observers: Any non-Pacific states interested may send their observers to the deliberations of the organization.
D. Others. Because of politically delicate relations between the PRC and Taiwan governments, their participation in the organization may be somewhat premature at this stage of the proceedings. Nevertheless, if the member states so concur, both governments could be invited to send observers or become full members. However, their joint representation in the proposed organization is inconceivable, and the organization should be prepared to accept one state as a member to the exclusion of the other. The proposed organization should avoid, at all costs, a politicized image.

V. Objectives
A. The basic purpose of the activity for the proposed organization would be to facilitate economic, cultural, and other cooperation for the benefits of all participating states. Such objective goals of the Center emphasize long-range cooperation; nor are short-term and immediate material gains to be expected. Patience and endurance will ensure slow and evolutionary development of the cooperative scheme.
B. In concrete terms, the objective of the proposed organization would not simply be confined to helping reduce the conflict among states in the Pacific. Rather, it should devote its energies to helping microstates in the context of North-South relations. In addition, the desired goal is mutual cooperation among developed states in the Pacific on matters of ocean resources, such as investment in fisheries and the mineral resources within the Exclusive Economic Zones (200-mile limits) of the coastal states in the Pacific.
C. In the initial phase of the proposed organization, the United States and Japan would take the major initiative in the creation of the proposed organization as major contributors to its funding. Simultaneously, other interested states would assume their share of financial contributions on an equitable basis. Perhaps the funding of the organization would be the most problematic, yet essential, ingredient for the succcess of the organization. Adequate consultation on this issue must commence before the proposed organization becomes reality.

Notes

1. Refer to Appendixes A and B for complete listings of Tokyo conference participants and the papers presented.

2. Garrett Hardin, "The Tragedy of the Commons," *Science* 162 (1968): 1234–48.

3. *Res communes* — in civil law, things in common.

4. *Res nullius* — *res nullius naturaliter fit primi occupantis*: thing which has no owner naturally belongs to the first finder.

5. First conference in a series of five, included in the Pacific Basin Research Project. The first workshop in Tokyo, held 25–28 June 1981, was entitled "The Management of the Pacific Marine Commons" (hereafter abbreviated MPMC.) This first workshop was jointly sponsored by the International House of Japan, the Aspen Institute for Humanistic Studies, and the Hubert H. Humphrey Institute of Public Affairs.

6. J. F. Kirk, "Energy Problems and Growth Prospects of the Pacific Basin," p. 5. Paper read at the Fourteenth General Meeting of the Pacific Basin Economic Council in Hong Kong, 4–7 May 1981. Kirk is chairman and managing director of Esso Australia, Ltd.

7. William H. Avery, "OTEC Methanol: A New Approach," p. 1. Paper read at International Resource Conference on Pacific Resources, Honolulu, Hawaii, 13–15 Oct. 1981.

8. Ibid., p. 8.

9. Third United Nations Conference on the Law of the Sea (hereafter abbreviated UNCLOS III), *Draft Convention on the Law of the Sea*, 1 Oct. 1981. (A Conf. 62/L.78) Reproduced by Office of Ocean Law and Policy, Department of State, Washington, D.C.

10. Dr. Frances Lai, "ASEAN's Perspectives on Managing Pacific Basin Marine Resources: The Case of Energy Development," pp. 20–23. Paper read at MPMC workshop.

11. Kent M. Keith, "Marine Mining: Six Scenarios for the Eighties," pp. 1–8. Paper read at MPMC workshop.

12. Quote by Ambassador T.T.B. (Tommy) Koh, taken from a press release entitled *Press Conference by President of Law of the Sea Conference*, 17 April 1981, p. 2. Ambassador Koh is currently Singapore's ambassador to the United Nations as well as President of the UNCLOS III negotiations.

13. Hardin, "Tragedy of the Commons," pp. 1234–48.

14. Daniel Behrman, *Genius of the Sea: John Isaacs* (New York: Simon & Schuster, forthcoming), p. 256.

15. UNCLOS III, Article 62:3, p. 24

16. UNCLOS III, Article 69:1, p. 27

17. UNCLOS III, Article 70:1, p. 28

18. Dr. Choung Il Chee, "Sharing of Fisheries Resources Between the Coastal and Other States: Towards Equity," p. 2. Paper read at MPMC workshop.

19. Ibid., pp. 5–6.

20. Ibid., pp. 9–10.

21. Ibid., pp. 12–13.

22. Peter Wilson, "The Views of the Pacific Island Nations on the Development of the Fisheries Resources of the Western and Central Pacific Ocean," p. 2. Paper read at MPMC workshop.

23. Ibid., p. 5–7.

24. UNCLOS III, Article 17, p. 6.

25. Ibid., Article 21:2, p. 8.

26. Ibid., Article 220:2, p. 91.

27. Ibid., Article 220:6, p. 92.

28. Edgar Gold, "Marine Transportation in the Pacific," pp. 6–9. Paper read at MPMC workshop.

29. Ibid., p. 2.

30. Ibid., pp. 3–6.

31. Hardin, "Tragedy of the Commons," p. 1244.

Bibliography

d'Arsonval, A. 1881. Utilization des forces natureles. L'avenir de l'electricite. *La Revue Scientifique*, 370-72.

Avery, W.H. 1981. OTEC methanol: a new approach. Paper read at International Resource Conference on Pacific Resources, University of Hawaii, Honolulu, Hawaii, 13-15 Oct. 1981.

Avery, W.H.; Dugger, G.L.; and Francis, E.D. 1980. Comparison of cost estimates, sharing potentials, subsidies, and uses of OTEC facilities and plantships. In *Seventh Ocean Energy Conference—Expanded Abstracts*. Washington, D.C.

Barnett, A.D. 1977. *China and the major powers in East Asia*. Washington, D. C.: Brookings Institution.

_____. 1981. *China's economy in global perspective*. Washington, D.C.: Brookings Institution.

Behrman, D. Forthcoming. *Genius of the sea: John Isaacs*. New York: Simon & Schuster.

Cohen, R. 1978/80. Energy from ocean thermal gradients. *Oceanus* 22:4, 12-22.

Craven, J.P., and Allens, S., eds. 1978. *Alternatives in deep sea mining*. Honolulu: University of Hawaii Press.

Dunbar, L.E. 1980. Market potential for OTEC in developing nations. La Jolla, Calif.: Science Applications Incorporated, in-house publication.

Gamble, J.K., Jr., ed. 1979. *The law of the sea: neglected issues*. Honolulu: University of Hawaii Press.

Gibbs & Cox, Inc., ed. 1980. *Seventh Ocean Energy Conference—Expanded Abstracts*. Washington, D.C.

Hardin, Garrett. 1968. The tragedy of the commons. *Science* 162:1234-48.

Homma, T., and Komogawa, H. 1979. An overview of the Japanese OTEC development. In *Proceedings, Sixth OTEC*

Conference, 19–22 June 1979. Gordon Dugger, ed. Washington, D.C.: U.S. Government Printing Office.

Kent, George. 1980. *The politics of Pacific island fisheries.* Boulder, Colo.: Westview Press.

Kirk, J.F. Energy problems and growth prospects of the Pacific basin. Paper read at the 14th General Meeting of the Pacific Basin Economic Council, 4–7 May 1981, Hong Kong.

Knight, H.G.; Nyhart, J.D.; and Stein, R.E. 1977. *OTEC legal, political, and institutional aspects.* Published under the auspices of the American Society of International Law. Lexington, Mass.: Lexington Books, D. C. Heath and Company.

Komogawa, H. 1980. OTEC for the Pacific islands—a Japanese perspective. Paper read at the National Conference on Renewable Energy Technologies, 8–10 Dec. 1980, University of Hawaii/Department of Energy, Honolulu, Hawaii.

National Research Council. 1979. Alternative energy demand futures to 2010. Washington D.C.: National Academy of Sciences.

National Research Council. 1979. Energy supply prospects to 2010. Washington, D.C.: National Academy of Sciences.

National Research Council. 1980. Refining synthetic liquids from coal and shale. *Final Report of the Panel on Research and Development Need in Refining of Coal and Shale Liquids.* Washington, D.C.: National Academy of Engineering.

Passin, H., ed. 1975. *American assembly: the United States and Japan.* 2nd revised edition. Washington, D.C.: Columbia Books.

Passin, H., and Iriye, A., eds. 1979. *Encounter at Shimoda: search for a new Pacific partnership.* Boulder, Colo.: Westview Press.

Ridgway, S.L.; Hammond, R.P.; and Lee, C.K.B. April 1980. Mist flow ocean thermal energy process. Marina del Rey, Calif.: R&D Associates, RDA-TR-110901-001, ORNL-7613.

Rochlin, G.I. 1977. Nuclear waste disposal: two social criteria. *Science* 195:23–31.

Scalapino, R.A. 1975. *Asia and the road ahead: issues for the major powers.* Berkeley: University of California Press.

Tokyo Electric Power Services Co., Ltd. 1980. OTEC. Tokyo: TEPSCO, in-house publication.

Trimble, L.C., and Potash, R.L. 1979. OTEC goes to sea. In *Proceedings, Sixth OTEC Conference*, 19–22 June 1979. Gordon Dugger, ed. Washington, D.C.: U.S. Government Printing Office.

United Nations. 1981. *Draft Convention on the Law of the Sea.* Third United Nations Conference on the Law of the Sea, Resumed Tenth Session, Geneva, 3–28 August 1981. Washington, D.C.: Office of Ocean Law and Policy, Department of State.

Whiting, A.S., and Dernberger, R.F. 1977. *China's future: foreign policy and economic development in the post-Mao era.* New York: McGraw-Hill.

Yuen, P.C. October 1981. Ocean thermal energy conversion: a review. Honolulu: Hawaii Natural Energy Institute, University of Hawaii.

Abbreviations

Amoco	Standard Oil of Indiana (U.S.A.)
ASEAN	Association of Southeast Asian Nations
BTU	British thermal unit
DOMCO	Deep Ocean Mining Company (Japan)
EEC	European Economic Community
EEZ	200-mile Exclusive Economic Zone
FBI	Federal Bureau of Investigation (U.S.A.)
FCMA	Fisheries Conservation Management Act (U.S.A.)
GNP	gross national product
ICLARM	International Center for Living Aquatic Resources Management (Manila, Philippines)
IMCO	Inter-Governmental Maritime Consultative Organization (Canada)
INCO Ltd.	International Nickel Corporation (Canada)
LNG	liquid natural gas
mile	nautical mile
MPMC	"The Management of the Pacific Marine Commons," Tokyo Workshop, 25–28 June 1981
OECD	Organisation for Economic Co-operation and Development
OMA	Ocean Mining Associates (U.S.A.)
OMCO	Ocean Minerals Company (U.S.A.)
OMI	Ocean Management, Inc. (Canada)
OPEC	Organization of Petroleum Exporting Countries
OTEC	ocean thermal energy conversion
PRC	People's Republic of China
quad	one quadrillion British thermal units
SCWRRP	Southern California Water Resources Research Project (U.S.A.)
Sohio	Standard Oil of Ohio (U.S.A.)

SSP	semisubmerged platform or semisubmerged platform ship
TRW	TRW Inc. (U.S.A.) (formerly Thompson-Ramo-Wooldridge)
UNCLOS III	Third United Nations Conference on the Law of the Sea
UNCTAD	United Nations Conference on Trade and Development

Index